# JEFFREY

## A MOTHER ENCOUNTERS THE INJUSTICE OF MURDER

*Book One of*
***The Next Day Came*** *Trilogy*

## K.D. WAGNER, MA
GOLD STAR MOTHER

# Thank You for Purchasing

# JEFFREY
A MOTHER ENCOUNTERS THE INJUSTICE OF MURDER

## SPECIAL FREE BONUS GIFTS FOR YOU:

Sign Up at **kdwagner.com** to receive
*UPDATES* and *RELEASE DATES* for:

*Book Two of*
*The Next Day Came Trilogy:*

# BUD
HOMICIDE TURNS A MOTHER'S BLUE STAR GOLD

Go To: **kdwagner.com**

Put Your eBook or Kindle Receipt Number for your
Book Order from Amazon or wherever you buy:

Order Receipt Number: _____

Your Name: _____

Email Address: _____

SIGN UP: for an AUTOGRAPHED "Hard Cover" Book for You or Someone you Know who would receive help from these stories. Meet **K. D. Wagner** on a *"Personal"* ZOOM Call Revolutionizing the "Online" Book Signing EVENT at:
**kdwagner.com**

Copyright © 2020 by Kathleen L. Dart Wagner

**JEFFREY**

All rights reserved. No part of this publication may be reproduced, distributed, or transmitted in any form or by any means, including photocopying, recording, or other electronic or mechanical methods, without the prior written permission of the publisher, except in the case of brief quotations embodied in critical reviews and certain other noncommercial uses permitted by copyright law. For permission requests, write to the publisher, addressed "Attention: Permissions Coordinator," at info@beyondpublishing.net

Quantity sales special discounts are available on quantity purchases by corporations, associations, and others. For details, contact the publisher at the address above.

Cover Art: *Black Birds Singing in the Dead of Night*
Artist: Sarah Stone at *sarahstoneart.com*

The author and the editor have tried to recreate events, locales, and conversations from the author's memories of them. In order to maintain their anonymity and to protect the privacy of individuals in several instances the names of individuals and places were changed as well as some identifying characteristics and details such as physical properties, occupations, and places of residence.  Any resemblance to actual living persons is purely coincidental.

Orders by U.S. trade bookstores and wholesalers. Email info@BeyondPublishing.net

The Beyond Publishing Speakers Bureau can bring authors to your live event. For more information or to book an event contact the Beyond Publishing Speakers Bureau speak@BeyondPublishing.net

The Author can be reached directly at meetme@kdwagner.com

Manufactured and printed in the United States of America distributed globally by BeyondPublishing.net

New York | Los Angeles | London | Sydney

ISBN Hardcover: 978-1-735558-92-9

ISBN Softcover: 978-1-952884-54-2

*To my sons, Bud and Jeffrey, whose lives and losses made me the person I am today, and to my love, Kim, who convinced me to stick around, heal, and write this story.*

# TABLE OF CONTENTS

PART I—Beginnings and Endings — 15
   Chapter 1: Living the Dream — 17
   Chapter 2: Scaling the Mountain — 22
   Chapter 3: Bad News and Nightmares — 25
   Chapter 4: Lost and Alone — 28
   Chapter 5: Questions with No Answers — 31
   Chapter 6: Let the Games Begin — 34
   Chapter 7: How We First Got the News — 38
   Chapter 8: The News Spread — 41
   Chapter 9: No Warnings Given — 43
   Chapter 10: Smokin' Down the Mountain — 45
   Chapter 11: Murdered—Day Two — 49
   Chapter 12: Devil in the Details — 51
   Chapter 13: Funeral Homes Suck — 56

PART II—The Beginning of Jeffrey — 61
   Chapter 14: Jeffrey's Life Began — 63
   Chapter 15: Life on the Rock — 75
   Chapter 16: A Unique Dude — 80
   Chapter 17: Meet My Parents — 87
   Chapter 18: My Mother's Words — 90
   Chapter 19: The Downward Slide — 92
   Chapter 20: The End of My Rope — 100
   Chapter 21: Attitude Adjustment — 103
   Chapter 22: Summer Vacation — 111
   Chapter 23: Peace and Happiness — 115

Chapter 24: Nothing Lasts Forever — 123
Chapter 25: The Soul Train Rolling — 129

PART III—Jeffrey's Never Coming Home — 133
Chapter 26: The Twilight Zone — 135
Chapter 27: Police Incompetency — 143
Chapter 28: Will This Nightmare End? — 148
Chapter 29: Lost in Limbo — 152
Chapter 30: Official Report — 158
Chapter 31: Flashback — 160
Chapter 32: Back to Work — 163
Chapter 33: Jeffrey's Home — 170
Chapter 34: Huge Expensive Vacation — 172
Chapter 35: Honoring Jeffrey — 175
Chapter 36: The Prosecutor — 183
Chapter 37: Sentenced. So What? — 191
Chapter 38: Love Stories and Backstabs — 198
Chapter 39: Birthdays Without Jeffrey — 207
Chapter 40: Life Goes On — 210
Chapter 41: Doctors and More Doctors — 222
Chapter 42: Promises Made — 230
Chapter 43: Lessons Learned — 241

Conclusion — 245
Next Steps — 249
About the Author — 250

# ACKNOWLEDGMENTS

Bud and Jeffrey are the sons I never dreamt I would have. After my childhood, I never wanted children. Their love, on both sides of the lifeline, taught me how to live, laugh, and love. They are forever in my heart. As Guardian Angels, they helped me to write this book.

Kim Wagner came into my life before the Universe took my sons. Her love, encouragement, and enduring patience allowed me to tell this story and write these books. She became my strength when I had none—the reason I stuck around long enough to heal—and she helped me become the person I was meant to be. I owe her my life, and eternal love.

To anyone who suffered a loss of a child, please know I understand to the depths of my soul the pain and sorrow you endure. There is nothing that compares to the loss of a child; it is the ultimate loss. I honor you in taking the time to read this story and walk with me through the journey.

Truthfully, a loss is a loss. The loss of a loved one, a relationship, a career, or a pet all hurt. No matter the loss, the process of grief needs walked through to survive. That walk is different for everyone. To heal, one must walk through the pain, find the purpose in that pain, and transform that purpose into a new passion.

I would like to thank the following people for their support and love during my loss, healing, and growth as I moved from grief to the writing of these books: first and foremost, my editor, Karen Burton, who made these books a reality; Marisol Velazquez and Joaquin, my adopted daughter and grandchild; and Matthew Seliski, my adopted son. Also, I would like to thank Leanne VanCamp, Lenita Lane, Nancy and John Wagner, Orly Amor, Julie Kessel, MD, Pam Lesher, Hope Hoch,

Ida Lazar, Sally Jo Hood, Marge Keyes, Julie Arenstein, Richard and Kathy Wagner, Robert and Judy Wagner, Brian and Jane Tattersall, Pat Morrissey, Eleanor Gabardi, Renea Lucci, Deborah Parsons, PhD, Julie Humphrey Thometz, Erin Teegarden-Wolbeck, PhD, Esther Martinez, Christine Beverly Thomas, Sandy Goss, Amy Luce, Jennifer Schiavone, Kevin Kellin, Jackie Bonafonte, JoAnn Zielinski, Becky Norwood, Natalie McQueen, Heshie Segal, Shannon Gronich, Tami Patzer, Sonya Nagy and Alain Barbera, Dr. Bob and Charlene Levine, Joy Grace Harmony, Keith and Maura Leon, Gary Coxe, Yolanda Mercado, Myrtice Landers, Roberta Brockway, Jean Uffalussy, Melissa Caratelli, Craig and Toni Gross, Rockie Lynne, Chris Marcelle, Alison M. Wheeler, and Adam Bricker.

*Every life leaves a mark on someone!*

~ Unknown

# INTRODUCTION

I am not dead, but both my sons are. In fact, it has been 6127 days since two separate events changed my life forever. The myth that *time heals all wounds* did not prove to be true. Time had passed me by. *The Next Day Came*, and I traveled through hell and back. I continued to live in that new life. There were countless days I did not want to be here on this Earth at all. On those days, I planned my exit. I was stuck in time, a living nightmare.

It was one of those days in 2004, when Kim, my spouse, convinced me that her God had a huge purpose for me to fulfill. She told me I just needed to hang on and heal, so I stayed. The knowledge I learned along the way was so worth the journey. Time, instead of healing my wounds, offered me a choice: how to find a Different Place.

Today is Super Bowl Sunday, February 4, 2018. The sun is shining in Santo, Florida. There is not a single cloud in the beautiful turquoise blue sky. The sliding glass doors are open to the pool area, and the warm air swirls around me.

Our house is full of life as people gather to watch the Philadelphia Eagles and the New England Patriots football teams battle on our seventy-five-inch large screen television. Kim loves people and parties, so conversations and laughter flow freely, along with food and alcohol. Everyone appears to be having a wonderful time.

Sitting in my recliner, I am in the room with twenty-five people, but alone, as my thoughts wander back over the years. The conversation and laughter swirl around me, but I do not understand any of it.

Something strange stirs in my soul. I quietly pick up my laptop computer and open a Word document. My fingers begin to move. At the top of the page, I type the words: Chapter One.

As the words begin to flow like rapids roaring down a raging river, I question myself. Am I writing this story, or are my sons, up in heaven, telling their stories through me? Whatever the reason, I let the words reveal themselves. I know these words have waited a long time to touch the light.

# PART I
# BEGINNINGS AND ENDINGS

CHAPTER 1

# LIVING THE DREAM

After ten years as a professional truck driver, I appreciated an evening drive out of Fallen Meadow, Utah, with no traffic congestion. I set the cruise control at 72 mph on the truck and turned on the current audiobook, which kept my mind busy while driving. Leaning back into my seat, I settled in for the long drive back to Rancho Santiago, California.

**My Family**

As the miles went by, I looked at my watch and surprisingly realized it was Wednesday, March 28, 2001, at 5:00 p.m. Funny, my younger son, Jeffrey, who lived in Fallen Meadow, had not called me. We had spoken the previous Friday on the phone for over an hour. Jeffrey and I always shared long conversations. One thing from that conversation kept running through my mind.

*Jeffrey*

Jeffrey had said, "Mom, I'll call you Monday. I've been thinking about it, and I want to move to California with you and Kim."

The week slipped by me, but Jeffrey never forgot to call me. We talked two or three times a week.

I said aloud, "How odd that Jeffrey did not call me. He seemed so excited."

JEFFREY | 17

I decided to call Jeffrey when I stopped for food and fuel.

My partner Kim and I had been together for just over a year when we moved from Fallen Meadow, Utah to Captain Island, California, in January of 2001. Kim and I met, surprisingly, on the internet in late 1999. We became friends online first, as we both traveled during the week for work. It took about three weeks to meet in person.

When we finally had time to meet each other, I took my mother Melinda with me in case Kim turned out to be a crazy woman or something. However, Kim and Melinda hit it off right away. The following weekend, Kim moved in with Jeffrey, Melinda, and me in Bighorn, Utah. The rest, as the saying goes, was history.

*Kathy and Kim*

At the time of our move to California, Melinda was in Fallen Meadow at a rehabilitation center with a broken leg. We would move her later. Jeffrey did not want to move, so at eighteen years old, he decided to stay in Utah. I was not thrilled about his decision.

Convincing myself, I said aloud, "Jeffrey will be okay. He's an adult now."

Neither Kim nor I had ever lived in California, so we looked for a safe place to rent. We found a gated community that allowed dogs. We had a six-pound poodle named Angel.

Not long after we settled into our new home, my oldest son, Bud, called from the East Coast of the United States. He had completed his four-year active duty commitment with the U. S. Navy and thought he would stay there for a while.

Bud asked, "Mom, I am buried in snow. Can I move to California and live with you and Kim for a while?"

I said, "Yes!"

Bud still owed the Navy four-years of reserve duty, but he could complete that in California. I believed the main reason he wanted to move to California involved Marisol, his soon to be fiancé. She lived in La Entrada, California, a suburb of Poison Oak. They met when Bud was on active duty on the East Coast.

Bud put his 1969 Chevy Nova onto a tractor-trailer and shipped it to California. He loaded up his 1986 Mustang with his belongings and strapped his surfboard to the roof. What a sight that must have been in a blizzard, as he headed off toward the warmth and sunshine of California.

Spending time with my sons filled my heart with joy. There were no words that described the relationship we shared. I divorced their father when Bud was three and Jeffrey was eight months old. As a single parent, I always worked hard to support my sons. I felt a huge responsibility to give them a better childhood than I experienced growing up.

*Bud*

I wondered: *Should I pinch myself? Could this be the happiest time in my life?* I finally found a partner with whom I felt safe and happy. Bud was coming home, and Jeffrey wanted to move home too.

For the first time in my life, I would have the loving, happy family I always dreamed of. I was living the dream, wasn't I? Heck, I even loved my job.

## My Career

My current professional truck driving job became a little complicated when Kim and I moved to California, but it was a good job that provided an excellent income, and I was not giving it up. I refused to lose my freedom. I drove a tractor-trailer, big truck, or eighteen-wheeler. I enjoyed my time alone, cruising the highways of America.

On Monday morning, March 26, 2001, I flew from Poison Oak, California to Fallen Meadow, Utah. I hopped on my Honda motorcycle, parked at the airport, two-wheeled it over to the distribution center, and started my week in my eighteen-wheeler.

During the week, I lived in my truck as it had a mini apartment behind the driver's seat. This included a twin bed, a chest for clothing, and a small television. There was a small refrigerator that ran off the cigarette lighter to keep my drinks and snacks cold. My home away from home.

The workers at the distribution center had my truck hooked up and ready to go when I arrived. I fueled up and headed to Rancho Santiago, California, where I set my alarm and caught six hours of sleep. At six a.m. on Tuesday, Wednesday, and Thursday mornings, I unloaded the 53-foot trailer full of frozen and non-perishable industrial groceries.

*Kathy and her Truck*

Each grocery item needed verification, separation, and distribution onto a separate wooden pallet for stocking purposes. Most trips, I helped to unload the 40,000 pounds of industrial groceries in the trailer.

Occasionally, I shocked people and unloaded the trailer by myself. This saved a trip to the gym, and it kept me fit and trim. I was 5 foot, 8 inches tall and 120 pounds of lean muscle.

The quicker my trailer emptied, the sooner I could head back to Fallen Meadow for a re-loaded trailer and the return trip to Rancho Santiago for a good night's sleep. As the saying goes, *rinse and repeat*.

## CHAPTER 2

# SCALING THE MOUNTAIN

On Wednesday, March 28, 2001, I was on my third trip back to Rancho Santiago, California, for that fateful week. I had forgotten to stop and get food while in Fallen Meadow, Utah. My mind focused on the drive, the intricacies of the climb up the mountain, and a trailer loaded with 40,000 pounds of groceries. This demanded my full attention.

My phone rang as I drove up the pass into the California desert. I did not answer my phone when driving, but I checked to see if the call was from Jeffrey. It was not. I really began to worry.

I said aloud, "Geez, Jeffrey never forgets to call me. I hope he's okay!"

The first call at 5:00 p.m. was from Artie, my ex-husband and father of Bud and Jeffrey, my two sons. We had not communicated in years. I doubted he called to tell me he wanted to pay me the thousands of dollars in back child support he owed. I had no interest in talking to him.

Not ten minutes later, a second call rang through. This time, it was one of Artie's seven sisters, Betty. This was bizarre. She had not spoken to me in the eighteen years since I had divorced her brother. She never liked me to begin with.

Neither call caused me any anxiety or a need to pull over and call them back. Climbing five thousand feet up a mountain in a truck and trailer loaded with industrial groceries, weighing a total of 80,000 pounds, afforded no time for phone calls, especially from ex-husbands or their sisters!

My truck had a governor installed that stopped the truck from going over 72 mph. My strategic plan was to reach that speed and hope nobody cut me off. If things did not go smoothly, and I had to slow down for any reason, the rest of the trip up the mountain would take forever and a day. At least it felt that way.

Even worse than slowing down was stopping a loaded truck going up a mountain. That equated to the kiss of death. Getting 80,000 pounds of steel to move again and back up to speed was impossible. Knowing this, the only reason I would stop was if the truck was on fire. Horrendous traffic, reckless drivers, and speeders made the climb a challenge every single trip.

I finally crested the top of the mountain into the Aha Makav Desert. It was a relief to level off on the flat of the high desert of California. Life became a whole lot less stressful for me. The rest of the trip would be smooth sailing until I dropped down into the Poison Oak Valley in three hours.

I engaged the cruise control, started my audiobook again, and sat back. There was nothing to do now but listen to my story, enjoy the ride, and relax. It was my last trip to California for the week. In two hours, I would stop in Waterman Junction, California. A bathroom break, fuel, food, and coffee were what I needed. Things had gone well this week.

*Kathy Driving Her Big Truck*

As a professional driver and a woman alone, I learned quickly where to find clean and safe restrooms. The Soaring K truck stop in Waterman Junction, California, was one of my preferred choices to stop. They were clean, well lit, and I always felt safe there.

CHAPTER 3

# BAD NEWS AND NIGHTMARES

Cruising along at 65 mph, still wondering about Jeffrey, I decided to wait to call him until I stopped for fuel. Unbelievably, my phone rang. This time, Kim was calling me. This was strange, as I always called her when I got back to Rancho Santiago and parked my truck for the night.

Somehow, I did not see the storm over the horizon when I answered my phone on March 28, 2001, at 6:00 p.m.

Kim abruptly asked, "Kathy, where are you?"

I replied, "The mountain pass, why?"

She asked, "Can you pull over?"

"No," I answered. "Why?"

Kim stressed slowly, "Kathy, please, can you stop the truck and park now, please!"

I have a tremendous work ethic. The importance for me to get to my destination and be ready for the morning unload took precedence over Kim asking me to stop my truck.

"No, Kim, just tell me whatever it is. How bad could it be?"

*Never ask that question.*

Slowly, Kim said, "Kathy, Jeffrey has been murdered!"

Time stopped. The world stood still. I could not breathe. My chest compressed so tightly that no air got into my lungs. *What the hell just happened?* I felt dizzy. I wondered if I would pass out. Would I vomit all over my truck? This was a nightmare. It could not be real.

I needed to breathe, but something stopped me. There was no air to breathe. Suddenly, I gasped and sucked air into my lungs. *Kim has lost her mind.* What the hell was she thinking, calling me, and telling me such bullshit?

I demanded, "What the hell did you just say?"

"Somebody murdered Jeffrey. They killed him in a robbery. You need to call a detective in Fallen Meadow." Kim replied.

"Are you freaking joking?" I demanded. "Where did you hear this crap?"

"Kathy, I promise, I will explain everything we know this far. Please just stop driving. Stop the truck!"

The realization that I was still driving a truck shocked me. By a miracle, I kept control of the tractor-trailer that was still traveling at sixty-five mph, locked on cruise control, down a busy freeway in California. Somehow, I managed not to harm anybody, including myself.

My Guardian Angels kept me safe once again. Through my tears and breathing convulsions, I saw an exit up ahead. I put on the turn signal and took the exit for Kelso Road. I stopped the truck and pulled the air brakes. The big metal beast no longer moved. *Oh my god, like my son, who no longer moved.*

"What the f**k? Murdered? No freaking way!" I yelled.

The taste of tears and snot filled my mouth. *How could this be?* I totally lost it. Alone, I sat in the pitch-black dark of the Aha Makav Desert, in the middle of nowhere California. My heart raced, my mind spun, and my head pounded.

I could not get enough air into my lungs. My body convulsed as I cried. Somebody must have reached into my chest and ripped parts of my body out, piece by piece. Had Kim really told me that Jeffrey died?

He was my baby boy. He was only eighteen years old. How could somebody murder him? The shock took hold of me. I went through stages of grief in minutes or seconds. Questions raced through my mind. *When, Who, Where, and Why?*

My body reacted as if it happened to me. *They* took both our lives. *Did I die? Am I dead? I must be dead, right?*

"Please, just let me die," I screamed. "Why? Why? Why? What the hell is wrong with this stupid f**ked up world? What have I ever done to deserve this?"

Between Kim's words, *somebody murdered Jeffrey*, and my thoughts that it could not be true, came the conviction that this asshole would die too. Only fair, right? Nobody murdered my child and got away with it.

"I will kill the bastard that did this. They will not get away with it. They better hope that the police shoot them dead, or they die in prison because I will hunt them down and kill them."

## CHAPTER 4

# LOST AND ALONE

There was a deadly quietness to the desert after I turned off my truck. It was so dark. I could not see anything. I felt like I was in a time warp. Everything was in slow motion. As I looked around, I realized I was in my truck and on the side of the road, but I did not recognize my surroundings.

My mind switched gears. I realized I was so alone. There was nobody who would come and save me. Nobody ever saved me. I was the one who saved everybody else. How would I continue to drive this truck? I could not move; I was frozen. Worse yet, somewhere, my child was cold, alone, and dead.

*While I drove this truck to California, somebody murdered my child.*

How could this have happened? What was I supposed to do? I knew there was something I was supposed to do. Suddenly, I realized I had groceries that needed to be in Rancho Santiago. Responsibility, browbeaten into me as a small child by my father, reared its ugly head. How could I worry about groceries when Kim said my child was dead?

Kim broke the silence.

"Kathy, are you there?"

"Yes. Wait, who told you this jacked-up information?"

Kim started to describe the phone call that Bud, my older son, received from his father, Artie.

"Wait!" I said. "Kim, I got two calls. It was from that ass. His sister. I did not answer."

"Yes, Kathy, when Artie called, and you did not answer, he called Bud. Without an ounce of empathy, he told Bud that Jeffrey was murdered."

"Poor Bud. What the hell?"

Kim continued, "Artie told Bud the Fallen Meadow Police could not find you. Somehow, they found Artie in Wisconsin."

That sounded crazy to me. Artie was never part of Jeffrey's life. He knew nothing about Jeffrey.

"Kim, why didn't the police call me?"

"Kathy, the police said they could not find you."

"How could police not find me? If . . . Jeffrey, my number in his phone, and police have my number from Jeffrey's juvenile record."

"Kathy, I don't know," Kim said. "The important thing right now is Artie gave Bud a phone number of a detective in Fallen Meadow. Kathy, you need to call this detective, as Jeffrey's mother, as soon as possible."

"Not calling f**king anybody. This is bullshit. Tell Bud I love him," I cried.

"Kathy, Bud is in shock. He looked so lost and confused when he hung up the phone. I told him I would call you. He is on the phone with Marisol."

"Tell him. I'll figure this out, I promise! Keep him with you, Kim."

"Kathy. I am so profoundly sorry. You love both your sons so much. You need to call the detective. As Jeffrey's Mom, the detective needs to talk to you."

"I can't. No! Jeffrey can't be dead? Who said? How do they? Are they sure?"

"Kathy, call the detective in Fallen Meadow. They can answer the questions you have. What do you want me to do?"

Sobbing, I snapped, "Bring Jeffrey back, not a damn thing. Nothing! Is there?"

"Kathy, is there somebody you can call, at your work, who can get you or the truck? Should we come pick you up?"

"Nobody ever helps me. Shit, why? I always fix shit," I sobbed.

"Kathy, are you sure nobody at your work can come drive for you?"

I replied, "Who? Who can I call? Always on my own. Why?"

"You are never alone, Kathy. You have Bud and me."

Defeated, I cried, "Whatever, give me the phone number."

They said Jeffrey was dead in Fallen Meadow, Utah. I would take the freaking truck back to the distribution center in Fallen Meadow. I needed answers. Kim gave me the number, but as I wrote the numbers down, my tears ran across the page. *Screw them all.* Disheartened, abandoned, and perplexed, I resigned myself to defeat.

I said, "Kim, I will call the detective and call you back."

With no idea of what to do or how in the hell to do it, I placated Kim and got off the phone. I hated that damn phone. I never wanted a phone to begin with and look where it had gotten me.

As the Mormons say, *my life went to hell in a handbasket.*

## CHAPTER 5

# QUESTIONS WITH NO ANSWERS

Back in the Aha Makav Desert, I have no idea how long I sat in the darkness. All kinds of questions ran through my head. What kind of awful, unfair world did I live in? What did I ever do to deserve this? Why would *They* take my baby boy from me?

Whatever the power of the Universe was, it was extremely horrible to me. My parents, from two different religions, never picked one to raise their children in, so we never took part in organized religion. Their God was a mystery to me.

However, I became a very spiritual person through my Guardian Angels and a power greater than myself, whom I chose to call *They*. To me, organized religion was a means to control people, especially women; therefore, I did not believe in organized religion.

The Universe was a power in and of itself. I talked to God, Spirit, Universe, whenever and wherever I wanted to. There was no need for a building, a book written by humans, or a man behind a pulpit telling me what to think or what I could or could not do. My brain and heart lead me throughout my life with kindness and love—I have no idea of its origin.

With no comprehension of time or place, I realized there was something I was supposed to do. I needed to call a detective in Utah. *Why could they not call me? Why on Earth would they have called Artie?* The police would never convince me they did not know my phone number.

*Can a person die of a broken heart? Where did I put that phone number? The police never even knew Artie's name or phone number, never.* None of this made sense to me.

In my mind, I decided the police made a mistake in the identification process. Jeffrey was not dead. I would prove it was not my Jeffrey. My mind swirled in anger and confusion. This police situation was not sitting well with me at all.

Questions swirled in my mind: How could a police detective perceive it obligatory of me, the mother of a murdered child, to hunt him down? Was detecting not the job of a police detective? Why should I call him, so he can notify me as the next of kin?

Follow the sequence here carefully:

1. I dialed the number the police detective gave to Artie, my ex-husband.
2. Artie gave that number to Bud, my oldest son.
3. Bud gave that number to Kim, my partner.
4. Kim gave the number to me.
5. Now, I had to dial the number to tell the detective I was Jeffrey's mother.

Honestly, I wondered how a detective could put my family through this kind of absurdity simply because he was unable to do his job—detecting.

Contemplate for a moment that they could not find me. I was a resident of the state of Utah. I previously was a sworn officer in the same police department in the state of Utah. I was a registered voter in the state of Utah. I was employed in the state of Utah. But they found Jeffrey's father, who had nothing to do with him and lived in the state of Wisconsin.

My family, from start to finish, received horrible treatment by the officers involved in Jeffrey's case. It started out with the absurdity of the notification process and quickly plummeted into an inhumane and outrageous chain of events. This was no way to treat a victim's family. The police never answered my questions about how they found Artie.

I digress. What I really needed was for the Fallen Meadow police to tell me they made a mistake, a horrible mistake, in the identification of the murder victim. I needed my baby boy, Jeffrey, not to be dead!

## CHAPTER 6

# LET THE GAMES BEGIN

I made the dreaded call. The phone rang and somebody answered. The person identified themselves by name and rank. I told them my name, and my mind slipped back into my officer academy training I attended all those years ago, after my divorce, when Bud and Jeffrey were children. I was not a mother nor the victim. The call became an officer to officer interview.

I asked, "May I speak to Detective J, please?" I waited.

"Detective J, may I help you?"

"I am Jeffrey's mother."

"Thank you for contacting me. I am sorry to inform you that Jeffrey was murdered in a robbery here in Fallen Meadow, Utah."

"Are you sure it is my Jeffrey?" I asked.

Unemotionally, Detective J said, "Yes, we verified his fingerprints."

I swallowed and took a deep breath. *Please let air get into my lungs.*

"When did this happen?" I asked.

"Monday, the 26th of March." He replied.

"Why am I just hearing about this tonight?" I asked. "It's Wednesday, the 28th!"

"We could not locate you." Detective J said.

"How could you not locate me? You are a police detective. Jeffrey's information is available through the Bighorn Police Department, Juvenile Hall, Hooterville Police Department, and I am sure the Fallen Meadow Police talked to Jeffrey. Did you look for my information?" I demanded.

"No, we located his father." Detective J replied.

I asked, "Why would you locate his father? There was no information about him on any record about Jeffrey."

Snottily, he said, "Well, we found you now, right?"

"No, actually, I found you. Where is Jeffrey?" I snapped.

"We released Jeffrey to a funeral home in Fallen Meadow. Where are you?"

"I am on the mountain pass in California. Why is Jeffrey at a funeral home?" I asked.

"They performed an autopsy at the medical examiners' and released his body to a funeral home until we located you." Detective J replied.

"Why couldn't you locate me? Jeffrey has my contact information."

"The person who killed Jeffrey took his phone and information." Detective J replied.

"What happened to his other belongings? Did they take his car? What about his passport? Did you find that?"

Monotoned, he said, "Those things must have been stolen."

My frustration level rose with this man. I was the victim's mother. I

JEFFREY | 35

asked, "What happened? How was Jeffrey killed?"

"We can discuss this in person when you get to Fallen Meadow," Detective J answered.

I replied, "I guess I will have to return to Fallen Meadow to get answers."

He continued, "You should be aware this crime has been on all the local television news stations repeatedly. Also, we have been asking for information on *Secret Witness/Crime Stopper* commercials to help us solve the case."

Shocked, I asked, "What are they saying about Jeffrey?"

"The television news has announced that an eighteen-year-old young man was murdered in a robbery. As his next of kin, now that I have completed the notification process, Jeffrey's name will be released."

His statement proved to me they wasted their time finding Jeffrey's father, as they could not release Jeffrey's name until they informed me. I was Jeffrey's next of kin. I gave up on that and moved forward.

I asked, "Do you have any leads or idea of who killed him?"

He blew me off again. He said, "We can discuss that when you get to town."

I told him, "I need to drive back to Fallen Meadow."

Detective J asked, "Is there anybody that can drive for you?"

"No, I am alone."

"Contact me again when you get to Fallen Meadow," Detective J replied.

That ended the call. There were just no words to describe the hell I was in. I promised Kim and Bud I would call them and tell them what the detective said. I did my best to relay the conversation with the detective.

Kim said, "Are you kidding me? That was horrible treatment."

Sobbing again, my body shook. I struggled to catch my breath.

Kim replied, "I assume you are going back to Fallen Meadow since that's where Jeffrey is, right? Bud and I will head for Utah when Marisol gets here. The poodles will ride with me. Bud and Marisol will bring his Mustang. I figured you and I will stay longer than they will, right?"

"Whatever. Back to Fallen Meadow. I don't understand any of it. Yes. No. I guess so. I have no idea. Keep me updated," I said.

"Kathy, do you want me to call Lynette? I'm sure we can stay with her."

"No. This is unbelievable. How? Freaking nightmare. I'll call. Whatever." I replied.

"Okay, we love you, Kathy. Please, take your time. Do not try to do what you cannot do. Please, I understand this is the most unbelievable thing, but we do not know all the answers yet." Kim said supportively.

I hung up and screamed at the top of my lungs. "I will prove that prick detective wrong. I will drive this freaking damn truck to Fallen Meadow and get answers. Jeffrey is not dead!"

## CHAPTER 7

# HOW WE FIRST GOT THE NEWS

Kim worked at home in Captain Island and traveled for her work. Her office was set up on the third floor of the townhouse, off the master bedroom. Luckily, she was home at 5:30 p.m. on March 28, 2001.

Kim finished work for the day and started down the stairs to the kitchen to make dinner. Bud joined her at the top of the stairs, as he would help her make dinner. Both my sons were excellent cooks. As they started down the stairs, Bud's phone rang, and he answered it.

Bud answered angrily, "Why are you calling me?"

Kim stopped and looked curiously at Bud. He motioned for her to go over to the table and sit down. She knew that whoever was on the phone, it was not good news. Bud looked visibly in shock. Bud hung up the phone, sat down at the table, and cried. Kim had never seen Bud cry before. His whole body shook.

"Bud, what is going on? Who was on the phone?" Kim asked.

"My asshole father said Jeffrey was murdered!" Bud replied.

"Bud, how on Earth would your father have that information?" Kim asked incredulously.

Kim did not have children of her own. She was not prepared for anything like this happening. However, she was a very caring and loving person, so she hugged Bud with everything she could.

Bud cried, "I . . . I wish . . . never took . . . call."

"Bud, I am so sorry you heard that news from your father like that. What exactly did he say to you?" Kim asked.

"He f**king just spit it out! Jeffrey murdered. Police can't find your mother," Bud replied.

"Oh my god," Kim said. "He just blurted out that Jeffrey was murdered?"

"Yes." Bud continued, "I asked, what the hell did you say?"

"Bud, what did he say about the police?"

"Cannot find my mother. Why not? Jeffrey has number. Don't have Jeffrey's phone. Won't tell him. What the f**k? Can't be true," Bud cried.

"Bud, how are we ever going to tell your mom about Jeffrey?"

"No idea. Need my mom."

"You know she usually won't answer her phone when she is driving," Kim said.

"Told. . . him, Mom call detective ASAP," Bud spoke through tears.

"Is that the information you wrote on the paper?" Kim asked.

"Yes."

"Should we wait until she gets back to Rancho Santiago?"

"No, tell her . . . she will be pissed."

Kim asked, "Was that all he said?"

"No, asshole on way to Utah."

"Bud, why would they come to Utah?" Kim inquired. "Your mom says he doesn't know Jeffrey."

Bud finally caught his breath and regained himself. "Kim, what the hell are we going to do?"

"I can't imagine what this will do to your mom."

"This will kill her."

"We have to tell her. There is no other way," Kim replied.

"What the hell? How could this happen?" Bud asked.

"Bud, I will call your mom if you want me to. It might be better if I tell her."

"Okay, please." Bud wept.

Kim suggested, "You call Marisol and tell her what happened."

Kim spoke while dialing, "Bud, I assume we will go to Fallen Meadow. That is where Jeffrey is, so your mom will want to go there to find out what happened to him . . . Wasn't it enough that my mother just died? . . . Bud, I absolutely dread making this call. If only we could be there in person to tell your mom. Who would murder Jeffrey?

## CHAPTER 8
# THE NEWS SPREAD

*As told by Marisol*

Sitting at my desk at work, strangely, my cell phone rang. It was from Bud. He never called me when I was at work, so I took the call.

"Marisol, someone murdered Jeff," Bud blurted out.

"What? Bud, are you sure? How do you know?" I asked.

"My father, asshole. Mom doesn't know. Somewhere in her truck. Kim trying to find her. Do you want to go with us to Fallen Meadow?" Bud replied.

"Wait, so your father called and said somebody murdered Jeffrey? Your mom is in her truck? Does she know what happened? I am so sorry, Bud. Oh my god, Bud, I can't believe this happened."

"Can you get to the house?" Bud asked.

"Bud, I have to go home and pack, then I will come to Captain Island."

In tears, I told my boss there was a family emergency and left work. I rushed home and packed my bag as quickly as I could. When I finally got to Bud, I jumped out of the car and ran to him. I hugged and held him as tight as I could. Together, we cried.

"Bud looks so broken and lost," I said to Kim.

Kim said, "We are all in shock. I can't imagine the state of mind Kathy is in sitting in the middle of the desert, in the dark, by herself."

"I agree, this is so wrong," I said. "Kim, thank you for thinking to have Bud call me. Of course, I'd want to be with him and you all at this time of crisis."

"Marisol, you are part of the family," Kim replied.

We got silently into our separate vehicles. Jagger and Angel, the two poodles rode with Kim. Together, we solemnly headed out on an unbelievably long drive to Bighorn, Utah.

"Marisol, how can Jeffrey be dead?" Bud asked. "He's only eighteen."

"Bud, I do not have any answers. Hopefully, when we get to Utah and find your mom, we'll be able to get the whole story. Maybe it's all a big mistake." I prayed.

Somehow, we would make it to Bighorn. Bud needed answers, and he knew his mother really wanted answers. Not knowing what happened was driving us all over the edge.

*How could it be possible?* Everything changed in an instant and forever in that one phone call from a man who never bothered to even know his sons.

"Why didn't they call my mom? Bud asked. "Why would the police call him of all people?"

"I don't know, Bud. I just don't know. I hope they are wrong."

CHAPTER 9

# NO WARNINGS GIVEN

March 28, 2001 at 7:00 p.m. Time was standing still, yet it was flying by, how could that even be? It had somehow been an hour since Kim told me my baby was dead. That fateful night, I sat alone in my truck. The desert was dark and cold. The realization hit me like a wall of ice-cold water. Shocked into reality, I realized I needed to do something. I wanted answers, and nobody was going to deliver them to me parked on Kelso Road exit.

No one even knew I was sitting there in absolute distress with the unimaginable knowledge that somebody murdered my child. The vehicles continued to drive by, oblivious to the collapse of my world only ten feet away on the side of a freeway. Nobody was going to show up to help me, so I needed to pull out my Super-Single-Mother strength and figure out what to do next.

It was time to call, Lynette. How would you tell someone their nephew was dead? *Wait, someone just called me and told me my son was dead.* So, I guess people could make those kinds of calls. Why should I worry about how this would affect her? I was tough; I took the blow. Well, she could take the blow too. The phone rang five times.

Finally, she answered. "Hey Kathy, what's going on?" Lynette asked.

"Jeffrey has been murdered." I blurted.

"What the hell did you just say? Are you freaking kidding me?" She asked.

"No, I am not freaking kidding! The detective said Jeffrey is dead."

"Oh my god," she said, "This is unreal. I can't believe it."

"Lynette, listen, I'm in my truck on the mountain pass. I'll have to drive back to Fallen Meadow. There is nobody to come get me or drive this truck. Can you meet me at my work and pick me up? I do not have a car. I flew in from California on Monday."

She answered, "Of course, absolutely, I'll meet you at the distribution center. Wait, where is it?"

"Kim, Bud, Marisol, and the poodles are leaving now," I said.

"How long do you think it will take you to get back to the terminal?" Lynette asked.

I cried. "Two hours, I don't know. What the hell? My head is going to explode."

"Kathy, before you attempt to drive that truck, get out, yell, scream, cry—even better—kick the tires, punch something. You need to get control of your anger. After you do that, then do it all over again. Get a bunch of that anger out of you, or you are going to implode. Then carefully, and I mean very carefully, drive that stupid truck back to Fallen Meadow. We'll be waiting for you."

"Okay. Jeffrey cannot be dead, can he? The detective was an ass. He wouldn't tell me anything. I don't get it." I stuttered.

I verified she had the address of the distribution center, hung up, and took her advice. It was a good thing I was in the middle of nowhere, in the dark, and by myself. People might have thought I lost my mind.

I yelled, cussed, screamed, kicked the tires, and punched the trailer. These things really hurt, but it did not matter; everything hurt. Then, I did it all again and cried some more.

CHAPTER 10

# SMOKIN' DOWN THE MOUNTAIN

Somehow, I managed to drive the 80,000-pound monster of rolling steel down the mountain without smoking the breaks. Even on a good day, if I rode the brakes going down the mountain, they would get so hot they smoked—and could even burst into flames. It had happened dozens of times.

The problem developed when an inexperienced driver panicked and stopped. Hundreds of trucks and trailers have burned to the ground when this happened. I knew the smart thing was to keep moving. The breeze usually cooled the breaks off and put the fire out.

Operating on remote control, as my mind wandered everywhere imaginable, I somehow made it down the mountain. It was truly a miracle that I managed to get the truck and myself down the mountain in one piece. Obviously, my Guardian Angels watched over me and guided the truck.

The last thing I wanted to do was cause anybody else to die. This trip down the mountain could have easily ended up with a big pile of metal at the bottom. In all honesty, I do not remember the drive to Fallen Meadow at all. My mind went over and over the things I had just learned.

Could it have only been a matter of an hour or two since I got the phone call with the news of my son's murder? There were thousands of thoughts about Jeffrey that swirled around in my head. I thought about his life and all the struggles we went through to help him grow up.

How was I supposed to think about his death? No, I was not going to do that. My mind protected me. Somehow it kept me sane enough to continue to function. Having driven this route at least a hundred times allowed my subconscious mind to keep the truck on the road and operational.

I pulled into the terminal yard in Fallen Meadow, Utah. I felt such a sense of relief. The tremendous responsibility of driving this 80,000-pound contraption on a public highway no longer weighed on my shoulders

**Responsibility First**

I saw Lynette waiting for me in her car. Thankfully, she did not get out of the car. Somebody was with her, but they sat and watched me maneuver my truck. I could not yet get out of the truck and go to her. I knew if I let go of my emotions for one second, I would never get back up again.

Still on autopilot, I completed the tasks I needed to do. I got out of the tractor and opened the doors of the trailer. I backed the trailer into a door of the terminal, pulled the air brakes, and took a deep breath. I verified all the paperwork and left it in plain sight for the manager to find in the morning.

I shut down the tractor motor and turned off the lights on the tractor and trailer. Lastly, I made sure the refrigerated unit was running on the trailer. This unit kept the food in the front of the trailer frozen and the rest of the food in the trailer cold.

Everything looked okay. I believed it would last until morning when the manager and distribution workers arrived. How or why I was able to think about all the things that needed completion before I left my work was truly a display of remote responsibility and integrity.

This phenomenal sense of responsibility, ingrained in me as a child by my father, who was a Marine Corps sergeant in his younger years, was one of the few good things I learned from him, but that needs to be a story for another time.

I gathered up my belongings and things I needed for the next day or two. I had no idea how long I would be at Lynette's condominium. I knew I could always come back and get something I forgot.

Lastly, I left a note for the manager on the window of the truck. I told him that I had a family emergency. I let him know I would call in the morning to explain. My subconscious mind amazed me, as this was all accomplished without thinking.

I surmised it was not a great idea to leave a note that somebody murdered my son, Jeffrey. The people at the distribution center had met him three or four times. Since the detective told me it was a big news story, it was more than likely they had seen the story on television.

It would be better to wait and tell them later. I would call them after 6:00 a.m. and tell them about the horror my life just became. It was more of a personal announcement, not something left on a note.

**Not Alone Anymore**

As I walked over to Lynette, I collapsed to the ground in sobs. Lynette, and her daughter, Lea, gathered me into their arms, and we cried. Finally, I was not alone; there was physical, emotional, and mental support.

Could they help me understand how one phone call destroyed my life? Could they make sense of what happened? Could they convince me that my life had not changed forever? I was doubtful, but they helped get me up from the ground.

Lynette said, "Oh my god, I cannot believe this."

"What did I do? Jeffrey did not deserve this."

"Kathy, you did not do anything to cause this. Neither did Jeffrey."

Lea said, "The story has been on the news repeatedly. I would have never thought it was about Jeffrey. Did they give you any details at all?"

"NO! I kept asking, but I have to call them in the morning."

Lynette said, "That is just unbelievable. I don't even know what to say."

Lea said, "I can't believe this happened to Jeffrey."

My two sons and Lynette's children grew up together. Now Jeffrey was dead, murdered. Surely, no family ever expected to experience the murder of a family member.

You read about it in the newspaper and hear about it on television, but you never realize how horrible it is until it happens to you and your family.

## CHAPTER 11

# MURDERED – DAY TWO

Lynette, Lea, and I arrived at the condominium in Bighorn, Utah. It would be three or more hours before Kim, Bud, and Marisol arrived from California. Driving that far in their agitated state of mind was one more thing for my brain to worry about. I made the same trip with extraordinarily little recollection of what happened. I could only hope they made it safely.

"Maybe it would be good if you tried to rest for a while." Lynette said.

"I doubt I will sleep, but I will lie down. This has been a horrible day. Tomorrow will not get any better, I'm sure."

"Kathy, you are probably right, I'm going to lie down. Wake me up if you need to. Love you! I am so sorry!"

She gave me a big hug and went to her room. Lea, who lived with Lynette, went to lie down too. The house got quiet, deathly quiet. I was alone again. My brain would not stop. How had my life changed in less than eight hours? How had the world turned upside down?

**Realistic Dreams or Nightmares**

I must have dozed off. Suddenly, I was in a vivid, life-like dream. Jeffrey pulled up in a pickup truck, which was strange, as he owned a car. He jumped out of the truck and walked towards me. You could always tell it was Jeffrey by his peculiar walk.

Jeffrey must have thought he was in trouble, as he wore that smirk on his face. He stopped right in front of me, looked me in the eye, and smiled.

He said, "I s'pose you're mad at me!"

Was it a dream, or had Jeffrey really come to visit me?

Growing up, Jeffrey always got this adorable smirk on his face when he knew you were mad at him. He said, *s'pose* not *suppose*. This might have been part of his dyslexia, or it was his cute way of getting out of trouble.

I sat straight up on the sofa. It was the end of my sleep. It was so real; it had to be a message. He was telling me he was still alive. The police were wrong, weren't they?

Since I could no longer sleep, I turned on the television. Unbelievably, the *Crime Stopper* commercial played on the television. Loud and clear, they broadcasted Jeffrey's name and asked for information about his murder. My heart about stopped.

"Breathe Kathy, breathe," I said aloud.

Seeing a television news *Special Report* broadcasting your child's description connected to the words, *murdered in a robbery* was indescribable. The news reporter asked for information on the man that killed Jeffrey. That just made my head spin. I felt nauseated. I was sure I would throw up.

As I laid on the sofa, I could not wait for the sun to come up. I wanted so much to prove that arrogant detective wrong when I showed them it was not my Jeffrey at that funeral home.

Since I could not sleep, I thought back on Jeffrey's life. I started with the day he was born and worked my way forward. I wanted to cherish every single memory I could conjure up.

## CHAPTER 12

# DEVIL IN THE DETAILS

March 29, 2001, 4:00 a.m. It was now day two of a word I never expected to have in my life, the *murder* word. Kim, Bud, Marisol, and the poodles finally arrived at Lynette's condominium. We hugged, cried, talked, and then we did it all again. Nobody had any answers, but everybody had questions, dozens of questions. We were all stuck in the unknown.

The three of them tried to rest for a while, but nobody was able to slow their minds down long enough to sleep. It was not long before we were all up again. Everybody showered and we tried to eat something. Mostly, we drank coffee. That was the best we could do. Lynette kept the cups full for us.

Kim and Lynette started with phone calls to family and friends. Somebody needed to tell people Jeffrey was dead. Guaranteed, it would not be me making those phone calls. I made one phone call, and that was to my work.

I talked to the manager, Bob. "Bob, I had to return to the terminal early this morning for a family emergency. Somebody murdered my son Jeffrey, in Fallen Meadow. You might have seen the news reports and *Secret Witness* reports about an eighteen-year-old murdered in a robbery? Well, that was my son, Jeffrey."

"Oh my god, are you kidding? The young man who came here with you a couple times and unloaded trucks for us?"

"Yes, that was him. I just got to the mountain pass when they called and told me it was Jeffrey. I called a detective here in Fallen Meadow, and they notified me as his next of kin. Now his name is on the news. My only choice was to turn around and come back to the distribution center. I am sorry I could not go on to Rancho Santiago."

"Kathy don't even think about it. Is there anything we can do to help?"

"No, not right now, I am barely breathing, Bob. I must call the detective back and get more details. He would not tell me anything over the phone last night. I'll let you know when I find out more."

"I am so deeply sorry, Kathy. I will let the corporate offices know of your loss. Our thoughts and prayers are with you."

"Thank you, Bob."

Lynette's condominium quickly filled with family members. We told great Jeffrey stories. It was so hard to be The Mom. People expected me to be the strong one.

Unsure exactly where Jeffrey was or what happened to him, I took a deep breath. It took everything I had to stand and talk. I made the dreaded call to Detective J, again.

"May I speak with Detective J, please?"

"Detective J."

"What happened to Jeffrey. Are you sure it is him?"

"Yes, we have verified that it is Jeffrey."

"How did you identify him?" I asked.

"We used his fingerprints."

This triggered something in my brain from yesterday's conversation. How could the Fallen Meadow Police Department not find me for three days?

"So, you found his fingerprints in the system, but you could not find my information connected to him?"

"His fingerprints were on record."

People who say stupid stuff are a huge pet peeve of mine. This man frustrated me. Furthermore, he did not seem to care about me or my concerns.

"If you looked at Jeffrey's records, then you sure as hell knew my information. Never mind, where is Jeffrey?"

Detective J responded, "He is at Memorial Funeral Home. You can give them a call and arrange a time to see Jeffrey today."

I felt like I could not breathe again. I was not prepared to deal with that information. My brain would not process that, so I moved on.

"Okay, we will see Jeffrey. Now can you tell me what happened?"

"Jack Ashe shot Jeffrey in the abdomen with a sawed-off shotgun resulting in Jeffrey's death. Then he robbed Jeffrey of his possessions. We are searching for Jack Ashe, and when we find him, we plan on charging him with murder with a deadly weapon and robbery with a deadly weapon."

This news was brutal; there were no other words to describe it. I wondered if he had an ounce of compassion or empathy left in his soul. I doubled over in pain, holding my abdomen. How could anybody do this to Jeffrey? He would have given the person anything he owned. This did not make sense.

Something about this did not smell right, nor feel right to me. My gut told me there was way more to this story. I could not get it out of my head. My brain kept going to the thought of a sawed-off shotgun on Jeffrey's stomach. I felt like I was going to vomit. I broke out in a sweat; bile filled my mouth.

Questions raced through my brain. Oh my god, the unimaginable pain Jeffrey must have been in. Did he suffer? Did he want to tell me something? Did he want me to hold him and tell him that everything would be okay? Would he have told me goodbye? Did he want to tell me that he loved me one more time? Was he alone? Was he afraid?

There were no answers, and somehow, I knew there would never be answers. I took another deep breath and tried to find the strength everyone expected me to have. I swallowed and convinced myself not to throw up. I needed to ask the detective the rest of my questions. I found my voice.

"Who is Jack Ashe?"

"Jack Ashe is a known criminal. This is his fifth crime with a gun—first time he killed anybody. He is a known tattoo artist. Our investigation so far shows that Jeffrey and this guy knew each other."

"Fifth crime with a gun? First time he murdered somebody—that you know of anyway, right? Are you telling me that Jeffrey knew the person who murdered him?"

"Yes, according to the witnesses. We are still conducting the investigation."

"Jeffrey loved tattoos. So, if he knew him, it was about tattoos."

The detective said nothing, so I continued my questions.

"Where are Jeffrey's car and belongings?"

Once again, Detective J did not answer my questions. "Go to the funeral home and see Jeffrey. We can meet tomorrow at 1200 hours to go over the case. You can pick up Jeffrey's car, as it is not in evidence. His other belongings are held in evidence until the trial."

I was done with this guy for now; there was nothing else to say.

"Okay, we will go to the funeral home."

"Call me in the morning. I will give you the address."

I hung up and relayed the information the detective told me.

Kim called the funeral home and scheduled a time for us to go to see if this lost soul was really Jeffrey. How the hell did these people expect me to verify my child was dead? Jeffrey was not dead.

CHAPTER 13

# FUNERAL HOMES SUCK

My recollections of the funeral home are minimal at best. Rationally, I know that Kim, Bud, Marisol, and I went to the funeral home together. I have no memory of the funeral home's location, nor entering the building, or with whom we spoke.

There was a vague recollection of Kim being there with me. Alarmingly, I have no memories of Bud and Marisol being at the funeral home at all.

These were my recollections of the funeral home.

A man wheeled a body on a gurney, like they have in a hospital, into the area I stood. I recall being in a hallway.

The body was intimidating. Draped in white sheets, except for the face.

1. Approaching the body, I repeated aloud, "Please, do not be Jeffrey!"
2. I did not look at the abdominal section of the body. I knew the perpetrator shot the person in the abdomen with a sawed-off shotgun, which freaked me out.
3. I closed my eyes, took a very deep breath, and looked at the face.
4. IT WAS MY DEAR SWEET JEFFREY!
5. I could not get air into my lungs. I thought I was having a heart attack. The room spun and I could not find balance. I should have crumbled and died right there, along with my son.

6. Jeffrey was dead. Every time I blinked or closed my eyes, Jeffrey's face, surrounded by white sheets, had *burned* onto the inside of my eyelids.
7. Incredibly, he wore that *smirk* on his face. The one he wore when he said, *I s'pose I'm in trouble.*
8. "Did you put that smirk on his face?" I asked.
9. "No, it came naturally!" he replied.
10. POOF! The world went black.

That was the last thing I remembered at the funeral home. There was zero memory in my head after that moment.

I have no idea how long we stayed, or when we left. I have no recollection of how we got back to Lynette's home.

I later spent six months in therapy with a psychiatrist, Dr. Carston. According to her, I went instantly into shock at the sight of my dead child. She called this instantaneous post-traumatic stress disorder (PTSD).

She explained, "The brain's ability to blank out these traumatic, horrific memories is quite common. The brain will protect people from acute trauma or stress. This allows them to keep their sanity."

This made perfect sense to me when she explained it.

She recommended, "Anyone who loses a child, especially under violent circumstances, should seek professional mental health care immediately."

In that moment, I stayed upright and remained breathing, but I was beyond mental comprehension. Part of my soul died, and part of my heart ripped from my body when I saw my dead child. *I gave birth to, nurtured, and raised this beautiful child.* Now, a beast had senselessly murdered Jeffrey. *My Jeffrey is dead!*

The *Soul Train* thundered into Fallen Meadow, Utah. *Death #3* happened. *All Aboard!* The red lights flashed, and the gates crashed down as the *Soul Train* roared into town.

I associated the *Soul Train* with the big steal monster trains coming down the railroad tracks. My father drove those monsters right through the middle of the town I grew up in. He taught us kids to fear them and scared us to death. We were never to cross those tracks when the gates were down.

He threatened, "You will die if you go around those gates when they are down." In fact, he sang a song all the time to intensify the reality that the train would kill me.

*Peanut sitting on the railroad track, its heart was all a-flutter. Along came a choo-choo train. Toot-toot! Peanut butter. Squish. ~ Anonymous*

I equated trains with death and named them *Soul Trains*.

**Other People's Memories**

Since I could not remember anything else that happened, I asked other people what they collectively remembered. Their memories were quite different from my memories. For historical purposes, the following are their recollections.

Of course, Bud was devastated by the loss of Jeffrey, his best friend. Lost in my own devastation, pain, and despair, I regrettably remain unable to remember what occurred when Bud saw his brother dead.

I freely admit that not knowing what happened with Bud when he saw Jeffrey, was one more devastating stab to my heart, but it might have saved what little bit of sanity I had left. It would have broken whatever small fragment of my heart that remained to see Bud's pain and devastation.

According to Kim, Jeffrey was in a room when we saw him. She remembered that Lexie or Lea read a poem. She also recalled that Artie, and his wife Gail, were at the funeral home. She has a vague memory of Artie and me sitting at a desk talking to the funeral director.

Kim said, "Many tears were shed, and stories of love were shared about Jeffrey."

Another thing Kim remembered was we decided Lynette would pick up Jeffrey's ashes, as she lived in the area. Kim and I would not wait for the completion of the cremation; we wanted to return to California.

Kim said, "The world lost a wonderful and peaceful soul with the loss of Jeffrey."

Marisol said, "We sat at the funeral home for a while. People said wonderful things about Jeffrey and told stories I'd never heard before. I was not sure who the people were, but they loved Jeffrey. I do not remember how long we stayed."

Lynette said, "We led a celebration of life for Jeffrey. We all gathered at the funeral home. Me, my children, and their families were at the funeral home."

Two years and five months later, Wyatt apologized to me for the way he treated me after Jeffrey's murder. By that time, it did not matter to me one way or the other, but that is another story.

**Medical Assist**

Somehow, we made it through the night. After the tragedy at the funeral home, my state of mind was not good at all. Worried about my mental and physical health, Lynette and Kim contacted a local doctor in Bighorn who had previously treated me.

After Kim explained the situation, he prescribed Valium and a sleeping pill. These medications were enough for me to rest. He relayed his condolences to me. He felt so sad I lost a child, even more so because he knew Jeffrey and treated him when we lived in Bighorn.

Thankfully, everything went blank for the next six hours, and I slept. I am sure it was a combination of the medication, lack of sleep, and the trauma of knowing my son was dead and gone forever.

PART II

# THE BEGINNING OF JEFFREY

## CHAPTER 14

# JEFFREY'S LIFE BEGAN

Jeffrey was born on July 17, Bud's third birthday, in Tabor, Wisconsin. Bud believed getting a baby brother for his birthday was the best present ever. He was absolutely thrilled.

Personally, I was thrilled that Jeffrey was born, period, after being in labor for twelve hours with Jeffrey stuck against my pelvic bone. It was a relief when he made his appearance in the world.

Unbelievably, Jeffrey shot out like a bullet when he slipped down off my pelvic bone. Thankfully, the doctor was standing there and paying attention. He caught Jeffrey, or he would have landed on the floor of the delivery room.

Jeffrey weighed in at a healthy 8 pounds 6¾ ounces. Bud weighed one ounce more when he was born, at 8 pounds 7¾ ounces. All their other body measurements were the same. This created a unique bond between the two of them from the start.

**Medical Issues**

Unfortunately, like Bud, Jeffrey was born with a blood condition called A-B-O incompatibility. Artie's and my blood types did not mix. I was O+ and he was A-. Both Bud and Jeffrey were A+. Jeffrey quickly became jaundiced, and his skin turned yellow. However, Jeffrey's condition was far worse than Bud's had been.

The doctors at the country hospital in Tabor quickly decided that Jeffrey needed to be in a neonatal intensive care unit (NICU). The medical staff arranged to transfer Jeffrey and me to a NICU hospital in Northdale, Wisconsin. Upon arrival, they took Jeffrey and ran more tests on his blood.

The doctor said, "We are going to have to do blood transfusions. Jeffrey's bilirubin is off the charts."

Panicked and alone, I waited. Just before the transfusions started, the doctors checked Jeffrey's blood one last time. His bilirubin level stopped rising. They decided he would not need a blood transfusion. He did have to stay in the hospital under the UV light for a week.

The gynecologist evaluated me when I arrived at the hospital. I planned to have a tubal ligation after Jeffrey's birth. Unfortunately, his birth resulted in extreme damage and tearing to my organs, and the doctor would not do the procedure at that time.

He said, "I will do the surgery for you, but not for five months. You need to heal. There was extreme damage when your baby slipped off the pelvic bone."

Jeffrey and I, released from the hospital, went back to the farm.

**A Father's Philandering**

Unfortunately, I had found out Artie was having an affair when I was eight months pregnant with Jeffrey. As an excuse, Artie sold farm supplies to local farmers to "supplement our income." Occupied with a two-year-old and pregnant, it took me a while to realize that he was out until after midnight. Farmers were not up that late, nor were they buying farm supplies.

One night before Jeffrey was born, I loaded Bud into the car and drove to the next town, Scully. Artie's car sat in front of the local bar. Holding

Bud's hand, with my eight-month pregnant stomach bulging out, we walked into the bar.

We found Artie dancing with a young girl. In anger, I kicked him in the butt with my foot. We turned and walked proudly out of the bar and went home. When I got married, I thought it would be for the rest of my life. I took my vows of marriage seriously. I had heard from Artie's family for five years how my parents screwed me up by not raising me with organized religion.

So many arguments occurred over my pregnant stomach, and later over a nursing Jeffrey. They say that a child senses stress. Did it affect Jeffrey's life? I cannot honestly say, but it was ironic that Jeffrey's favorite statement was *F\*\*k It!* See his finger? In fact, this phrase started young and became a theme throughout his life.

*Baby Jeffrey - Middle Finger*

In December 1982, I was able to have the tubal ligation postponed at Jeffrey's birth. For once, a member of Artie's family stepped up, and his oldest sister, Gracie, came and watched the two boys while I went to the hospital.

My relationship with Artie was non-existent, but I knew I was not having any other children, no matter what happened in our marriage. I offered to leave the farm and go anywhere else in the country, together, so we could start again, but Artie had no interest in saving our family.

I stayed on the farm until Jeffrey was eight months old. Artie continued to go out and meet the girl named Gail. I told Artie I was leaving and taking the boys with me. He did not care. In fact, he left it up to me to tell his parents I was leaving. When I told them why I was leaving, they did not believe me.

Reba, Artie's mother, said, "My son was raised in the Episcopal church. He would never do such a thing. You will be back in six weeks. You will never be able to make it on your own with two little children."

I arranged for a moving truck to pick up our furniture and move it to Utah. I flew Lynette out to meet us in Red Water, Wisconsin. Together, we made the trip from Wisconsin to Utah. Bud, Jeffrey, and I moved into my mother's home in Bighorn, Utah.

Funny story. While Lynette and I drove to Utah with Bud and Jeffrey, Reba called Melinda.

Reba said, "Melinda, if you raised your daughter correctly, this would never have happened, and my grandchildren would still have their father."

Melinda was not happy about this at all. By the time I arrived in Utah, she was fuming. When Reba finally found out the truth, she called and apologized to my mother. Reba was after all, a god-fearing woman.

## New Beginnings

The world was a blank slate for the three of us when we arrived in Utah, but my life was certainly not how I planned it to be. I was a single parent, twenty-three years old, and had never had a real job, as I worked on the farm in Wisconsin. Divorced with a three-year-old and an eight-month-old baby, Bud, Jeffrey, and I grew up together. We were the Three Musketeers!

*Bud (4) & Jeffrey (1)*

We stayed with Melinda for a couple of months while I found a job and a place for us to live. This was quite an adventure, as my mother's house was already full. Mac, Lynette, and her children, all lived at the house already.

Lynette had been living with our mother for over three years at the time we came to stay at the house. With the addition of the three of us, nine people lived in a three-bedroom home. They made a makeshift bedroom for us in the game room. It was a large room with a pool table, off the swimming pool area. Jeffrey was still in a crib. Bud and I slept on couches.

I was still nursing Jeffrey, but I had to stop and put him on a bottle. I found a job, and that required a babysitter while I worked. Lynette and I took turns babysitting each other's children.

## My First Real Jobs

When I first arrived in Utah, my mother helped me get a job at the J Davis & Co. distribution center where she worked. They knew she was a terrific worker, so they gave me a chance. I proved to them that hiring me was a great decision. Sometimes, I worked two jobs. One of these jobs was delivering the Bighorn Newspaper.

The company tossed the unfolded papers into my mother's driveway at 3:00 a.m. every Tuesday morning. Melinda helped me. We got up, folded, and delivered the papers before we went to work at J Davis & Co. For this effort, I received $14 cash weekly, which filled my car with gas for the week.

Melinda always had her favorite child and grandchild. If you were the favorite, it was great. Lynette had been the favorite for years, along with her children.

Having been away from all my family and its dysfunctional ways for six years, I could not wait to get a home for Bud, Jeffrey, and me. The Three Musketeers needed a place of their own—and soon.

Bud and Jeffrey spent hours of their time in daycare and with babysitters. It was not the life I wanted for my two sons. Anger boiled in me at their father, and alcohol consumption cooled that anger down. I worked at J Davis & Co. for one year. The work was very physical but was not challenging me mentally.

## A New Career

After a year, I applied for officer training at the Fallen Meadow Police Department. I took all the required testing and made the list. The sixteen-week academy would be not only mentally challenging, but physically challenging too.

The academy started in July. The weather was hot, over 100 degrees every day. We ran for miles and did calisthenics on the smoking hot concrete of the parking garage roof at the county building.

They held the academy classes on the fourth floor of the county building. The elevators were for instructors only. The trainees ran up and down the stairs a thousand times.

Every night I went home and told Melinda, *I quit*. She told me no, you are not quitting. At 4:00 a.m., she got me up and sent me back to the academy. I finished second in my class of fifty officers of two women and forty-eight men.

As a Transportation Officer, I worked eighty-plus hours every week. The work was dangerous, and things could quickly get violent. There was a constant threat of danger, including death. I knew when I went to work that I might never come home.

*Officer Kathy*

They required me to sign a paper saying I understood there was a *no-hostage* policy. This meant they would not negotiate with the hostage-takers to save my life. Although I signed this paper to get the job, it did not sit well with me and swirled in the back of my brain. What position was I putting my two sons in if the inmates took me hostage or killed me at work one night, and I never returned home?

One of my jobs was to transport both male and female detainees to court. Sometimes, I sat at the hospital or outside facilities with them. One night, I even helped deliver a baby at the detention center as there was not enough time to take her to the hospital. It was a great-paying job, with impressive benefits; however, I was not happy at my work or in my life.

**Harassment**

An extremely negative part of working in this male-dominated job in the 1980s was unlimited nasty treatment, resentment, and untrue rumors. As a single parent with two small children, who was working eighty-plus hours a week, I had little time for a personal life.

However, when I got to work for rollcall, I heard all sorts of rumors about my so-called sex life. There was no rhyme or reason for which woman the male officers picked on. Divorces and marriages were rampant in the department, mostly fueled by unbelievable amounts of alcohol. People I did not even know spread rumors about me.

When I walked into rollcall, everyone pointed and laughed at me. I had no idea what they were talking about until later when a friend told me. It was ridiculous. If I dated one of them, I was a slut. If I did not date one of them, I was a lesbian. No matter what, I could not win. So, I worked, drank, and took care of my two sons.

## Increased Alcohol Consumption

This was not what I signed up for when I got married and had two children. I did the best I could under the circumstances, but it felt like I was drowning. My anger fueled unbelievable amounts of alcohol consumption. This job fed the consumption of alcohol, too. The rumors and reputation related to sworn officers and heavy drinking proved true repeatedly to me. I fit right in.

When the shift was over, there were always people going to the bar to dance and party. Thankfully, I was a highly functioning alcoholic, so no one knew the amount of alcohol I consumed.

Bud figured it out before anyone else. When we moved out of Melinda's house, the boys used to stay at her house when I worked long hours. Sometimes in the morning, when I woke up at our house, I would ask Bud how we got home.

"Mom, you picked us up at Grandma's last night, don't you remember?"

Unfortunately, I did not remember how we got home. Blessed, I never hurt them, myself, or anyone else in all the years I drank. My Guardian Angels always kept me safe. I focused on the two missions important in my heart. One was to support my sons, and the other was to never go back to Wisconsin.

## Stress Relief

When I was not at work, we found time for fun. I bought a twenty-one-foot ski boat. We kept the boat at Lake Elwood. Both boys loved the water. Once the boat was out of the harbor and past the no-wake zone, I was behind the boat on a rope and a waterski.

People thought it funny because when I came up out of the water, I carried in my swimsuit a comb to fix my hair and a can of beer to quench my thirst. Jeffrey too was always in style, but on the other hand, he thought the boat was excellent for napping. It never failed that he fell asleep on the ride.

There had to be more to life than working and paying babysitters. Between my work schedule, the stress of the job, being a single parent, and an occasional date, I was exhausted. One of my sergeants at work noticed I struggled with my work schedule and the responsibility of raising two sons.

**New Relationship**

One night, my sergeant suggested I meet his ex-son-in-law. The *ex* should have been my first red flag. Tired, overworked, and a large consumption of alcohol all played a factor in my desire for a way out of the mess I was in. Of course, I continued to blame it all on Artie.

My sergeant spoke highly of his ex-son-in-law, so I decided to take a chance and meet him. He was in the Marines, so I called him G.I. Ranger. At the time, he attended a school somewhere in Texas called Sergeant Major Academy. Knowing nothing about the Marines, other than my father, this should have been a giant red flag, so this school did not impress me. G.I. Ranger and I talked on the phone and wrote letters to each other. Yes, this was before computers, email, and texting.

When his graduation came around, he invited me to attend. I did not want to go alone, so I took Jeffrey with me to the graduation. He was only two years old, but he was happy to go with me. We flew to Texas. I was instantly fascinated with the military, along with the pomp and circumstance of the graduation ceremony. I later found out that attending this school equated to getting a master's degree.

Everyone was genuinely nice, and Jeffrey liked G.I. Ranger. He was attentive and loved children. We drove back to Fallen Meadow in his car and talked about our life stories. It was at this point I learned that G.I. Ranger had four children of his own, and he had custody of them. They were staying with my sergeant and his wife, their grandparents. This fact should have been my third red flag.

G.I. Ranger was fourteen years older than me. I hoped he would be more mature than the boys' father. When we got to Fallen Meadow, I met his children, and he met Bud. My sons got along well with his children. We spent a couple of weeks together at my mother's house in Bighorn, swimming, and boating on Lake Elwood.

G.I. Ranger received his next duty station orders in Hawaii for three years. This was a major attraction for me. I had always wanted to go to Hawaii. Years before, my mother flew Bud and me out to Utah from Wisconsin to babysit for Lynette's children and Mac, so that my mother, her second-husband, and Lynette could go to Hawaii on this huge vacation. I always felt slighted in that situation.

Melinda's *modus operandi* (MO): If you were her favorite, you scored.

To the shock of my family, when the marriage proposal came, I accepted it. I said *yes* to three years in Hawaii—not to love or a lifetime commitment. I had no idea what I had gotten myself into, and nobody had the balls to ask me.

**JEFFREY | 73**

Two of the girls I worked with planned the wedding. Believe me, law enforcement officers will party for any reason, but a wedding was one of their favorites. They consumed huge quantities of alcohol, and this celebration did not disappoint. Next thing I knew, Bud, Jeffrey, and I packed up and moved to Hawaii with G.I. Ranger and his four children. What a plane ride that was to the Islands.

## CHAPTER 15
# LIFE ON THE ROCK

When we were on the flight to Hawaii, the flight attendants probably thought their day had gone to hell. My law enforcement training helped me manage six children, ages seven and under. They all behaved, and the flight went fast.

While I had no problem with the six children, my new husband did. As we settled into life on the Island, reality started to rear its ugly head. When G.I. Ranger came home and found one of his children in a time-out, the shit hit the fan, as the saying went.

He said, "Why is my kid sitting on the couch while your kids are playing?"

I answered, "Because your kid just hit his sister over the head with a truck."

He told his child, "You can get up now. If they are playing, you are playing."

The kids and I did great. I loved them and they loved me. However, being married to G.I. Ranger brought back all the nightmares from my childhood. This time, I would not tolerate the abuse. I stood toe-to-toe with him and fought back. G.I. Ranger and I were the perfect couple with other people, but all hell let loose when we were alone.

## That Did Not Last

The beginning of the end happened at the Marine Corp Ball celebration when a couple of younger male soldiers flirted with me and questioned why I was married to an old man. That night, G.I. Ranger showed me, through assault, that he could do anything those younger soldiers could do.

There were no apologies. I threatened to go to his commanding officer, and he swore it would never happen again. That promise was short-lived, and the next time, after I learned he had shared a sexually transmitted disease, the violence escalated, including a hole he punched in the wall next to my head. That was the last straw. I reached my limit and planned my return to Utah.

G.I. Ranger and his ex-wife decided it would be better if their four children lived with her in Fallen Meadow. I flew home with six children. His children did not want to live with either one of their parents, but I was unable to keep them.

## Funny Story

On the plane ride home to Fallen Meadow, Utah, all six children, seated in the middle row of the plane, were reading. I needed to go to the restroom. I saw two ladies sitting in the row behind the children.

I asked, "Will you please watch the children while I go to the restroom?"

They questioned, "You will come back, right?"

I replied, "Where would I go?"

They laughed and said, "Okay."

When the flight landed in Fallen Meadow, the flight attendants gave me a huge bottle of champagne.

They said, "We thought this would be a horrible flight when you got on alone with six kids, but it was not a problem at all. I don't know how you trained those children, but you deserve this, enjoy."

**Crazy Is as Crazy Does**

Surprisingly, Bud, Jeffrey, and I left Utah, and went back to Hawaii after three months. In my alcohol-soaked brain, I decided being with G.I. Ranger was better than being alone. I had one screwed up head. After the abuse of my childhood, and two marriages, I deserved no more than G.I. Ranger—or so I thought. I was damaged goods. He convinced me nobody else would ever want me.

Bud, Jeffrey, and I loved living in Hawaii, other than my relationship with G.I. Ranger. He was a good father figure to Bud and Jeffrey. He taught them boy things. He took them camping on the beach and taught them to surf and fish. He must have missed his children. Bud and Jeffrey received the better end of my second marriage. They loved the military and wore camouflage outfits like G.I. Ranger.

Growing up, Bud and Jeffrey always received the same presents for their birthdays and Christmas.

*Jeffrey (5) and Bud (8)*

They received five or six toys and new clothes for the following six months. This worked out nicely, as they never had anything to fight about. Well, not really, but that was my principle.

**Alcohol Consumption and Escapes**

Bud and Jeffrey had a 7:30 p.m. bedtime. They read books when they went to bed. It was my time to relax and drink. Although I never drank in front of my children, my main escape from life with G.I. Ranger was vodka—gallons of it.

However, when I drank, I did not eat much. It never failed that when I got dinner ready, G.I. Ranger complained about something I had not done well enough for him, so I did not eat. I weighed 98 pounds, at five-foot-eight inches tall, by the time I left Hawaii three years later.

Another escape from my marriage was playing softball. I joined a group of military spouses at the Navy base. This gave me a physical and mental outlet. I met my friend Donna and her three children. Her husband deployed regularly in the Navy. We babysat for each other's children, went to the beach, and hung out together.

She and I are still dear friends today. Donna was one of the few people who witnessed the abuse I suffered with G.I. Ranger. She supported me through the issues the marriage caused me mentally and physically. She kept me alive when I reached the end of my rope.

**Vacations**

Occasionally, we made a trip back to the mainland. On one of these trips, we rode on an Air Force cargo plane out of the Air Force base. Bud and Jeffrey were thrilled; we sat in the net seats that the military personnel flew in.

There were no windows to see out of the plane, and there were no flight attendants. The restroom, for me, was an outhouse on a pallet in the middle of the plane. The male passengers used a tube to urinate. Bud and Jeffrey needed to pee ten times in a five-hour flight.

What an adventure for me and the boys. Bud and Jeffrey never forgot those plane rides. This later influenced Bud in his career choices.

*Jeffrey on Vacation*

CHAPTER 16

# A UNIQUE DUDE

Jeffrey was an old soul. He was very mature for his age. He sat like an adult and behaved better than most adults I knew. I described him as four, going on forty.

**Jeffrey Story**

However, Jeffrey was not perfect. One time at the Army hospital, he pulled the fire alarm in the doctors' waiting room. When the military police (MPs) arrived, Jeffrey's concern was that he would not get lunch before they took him to jail. The MPs explained the problems Jeffrey caused the hospital, Jeffrey apologized and promised never to do that again, and he never did.

When Jeffrey was three years old, I realized he was experiencing a learning disability by comparing him to Bud. I was not a medical doctor, but as his mother, I knew Jeffrey was different. At the age of three, Bud could spell and write everybody's name in our family.

Jeffrey could not write anyone's name. When we moved to Hawaii, Jeffrey told people he was moving to Hu-ha-wii. He spoke his own language. I understood what he said, but other people did not.

Jeffrey loved animals and asked for a poodle puppy. The lady said Jeffrey had to wait eight weeks. Jeffrey did not understand time. This was another sign of a learning disability. He kept track of time by the number of sleeps he needed before something happened. We used a calendar with red *X*s to keep track of his sleeps.

## Disability Testing

Finally, at the age of five, a developmental psychiatrist at the Army hospital evaluated Jeffrey for learning disabilities. The results of the testing showed Jeffrey's IQ was 163, in the genius range. However, he suffered acute dyslexia, with mirror writing.

Jeffrey printed his name as ffeJ. He not only reversed numbers and letters, but he also reversed syllables and wrote words completely backward. Nonetheless, through special schooling, and hundreds of thousands of dollars, he learned to read, write, and do math in a unique way, different from anyone I ever saw.

The psychiatrist administered a test to evaluate his attention span. The doctor asked Jeffrey to watch this machine and push a button when the red light came on. He pushed the button once in the entire test. After that, he turned the machine upside down and tried to figure out how it worked. The test revealed his attention span was fifteen seconds. They diagnosed him with attention deficit hyperactive disorder (ADHD).

With an understanding of Jeffrey's struggles, I promised this little five-year-old boy I would do whatever it took to get him through high school and into a job that would support him for his life. I am not sure he understood the scope of that promise, but he understood I loved him and would be there for him. That I was sure of.

## Never Peace in My Life

Unexpectedly, in 1988, I received a phone call telling me that G.I. Ranger aggravated an earlier injury he received in Vietnam while taking part in a training exercise on the Marine Corp base. As a result of this injury, the Marine Corp medically retired him. This was traumatic for him and our family.

Once again, Bud, Jeffrey, and I returned to Bighorn, Utah. G.I. Ranger and I rented my mother's house. Melinda had moved in with my granddad after my grandmother died.

Retirement did not sit well with G.I. Ranger, as he was no longer in command of troops, of me, or anyone. He quickly became dissatisfied with the civilian world. Even though he made more money, he was not in charge, and that just did not sit well with somebody who they considered *god* at his rank in the military.

Things were even worse in our marriage, and this led to innumerable arguments. One day, I came home from work, and G.I. Ranger was waiting for me at the front door.

He yelled, "You are not happy; I am not happy. Why don't we get divorced?"

"That sounds like a fantastic idea," I agreed, fed up with marriage, period.

This was not the response he expected, and it led to one of the biggest arguments we ever shared. It was a brutal, toe-to-toe argument, resulting in three holes in the walls of my mother's home.

G.I. Ranger demanded, "Who are you sleeping with? Who's the other guy?"

I replied, "I already have one too many assholes—why would I want another one?"

Finally, I reached the limit of the abuse I could, or would, tolerate and filed for divorce. I thought that would end the arguing. However, it took another year for the divorce to finally be over.

Every time we were set to go into court and sign the paperwork for the divorce to be finalized, G.I. Ranger decided he wanted one more thing from the house or one more condition met. It cost increased money and time with every delay.

G.I. Ranger finally quit harassing me when Renea entered the picture. I met her at a bar in Fallen Meadow one night after G.I. Ranger moved out. We became friends and dated off and on for years.

Renea offered, "Tell him I will slide the console television he wants down the two flights of stairs for him to pick up at his convenience."

With that, he signed the paperwork, and the judge completed the divorce. I wrote the whole marriage off to large consumptions of alcohol.

Truthfully, I learned things about myself. For one, I grew up. I realized it was better to be alone than abused and treated like crap. I also discovered I had two emotions that came out of my childhood—fear and anger—which ruled my life. I decided to spend time finding out who I was and what I really wanted in my life.

As the saying goes, *Hindsight is 20/20*. The marriage ended after six years.

**Divorced Again**

After the divorce, I continued to rent Melinda's home in Bighorn. Once again, I was raising my two sons alone. I needed to find a decent-paying profession. I took the test and received my commercial driver's license. During my six years on the farm with Artie, I had learned how to drive all sorts of farm equipment and vehicles. With a commercial driver's license, I found a job with a trucking company.

Unfortunately, this job took me out of town and across the country. Thankfully, my family watched Bud and Jeffrey. I did what I had to do to make sure Bud and Jeffrey had the things they needed and wanted. Unlike my childhood, I made sure they owned the right shoes, clothes, bikes, and things children used to judge each other by.

Bud and Jeffrey saw how hard I worked and how I lived my life with integrity and honesty. We were the Three Musketeers. We worked as a team. They learned how to cook, clean, and do their own laundry. As they grew into young men, they, too, were diligent workers. They helped anyone with anything needed.

Jeffrey was not a physically hyper child. He did not run around or act out of control. Distracted, he moved on to other things. The doctors placed Jeffrey on Ritalin, which the teacher did not feel helped him.

Later, as he aged, they placed him on Adderall and Dexedrine. I wish I had questioned the doctor about the long-term effects of these prescriptions. If I had, I would never have given Jeffrey these drugs, or any other drugs for that matter.

**Education Struggles Begin**

Jeffrey's education was a struggle both financially and emotionally for all three of us. Their father did not pay his court-ordered child support, so all the economic responsibility was on me. My children knew the truth about the decisions their father made, but I never bad-mouthed him.

Artie married Gail, and they never had any other children, nor did they have any relationship with Bud and Jeffrey. They did not send birthday or Christmas presents to Bud and Jeffrey.

The public-school systems did not provide Jeffrey with a proper education that addressed his learning disabilities. Nor did the government have any subsidies to help me with private education. Luckily, on returning to Bighorn, Utah, I found a private school that helped Jeffrey, and he received a scholarship that paid for it.

This school taught Jeffrey how to read and do mathematics with his dyslexia. He read the word itself from right to left and then read across the page from left to right. He learned to do mathematics in a way I never understood. Things went well for Jeffrey at this school.

*Jeffrey at School*

This school was a blessing to us as it gave Jeffrey the foundation that got him through all his schooling.

**Swimming and Disabilities**

Swimming helped Jeffrey with his learning disabilities. Both Bud and Jeffrey swam competitively throughout their school years. Swim practice was after school. However, Jeffrey did not attend public school. He always felt different because he arrived at swim practice later than the other children.

*Jeffrey Did Not Say It Was School Photo Day*

Even though Jeffrey did not like being different, he certainly had his own personality. He was sensitive, and thought the other kids talked about him. One thing that helped him win the other kids over was that he became an excellent swimmer and won innumerable awards.

Jeffrey continued to swim competitively and was able to burn off his excess energy. He won two prestigious plaques while in Utah when he competed in state championships. He took second place in the 7–8 age group and then again in the 9–10 age group.

## CHAPTER 17
# MEET MY PARENTS

When I came home from work one day in June of 1992, I turned the corner to see a *For Sale* sign in the front yard of my mother's house. Funny thing, she never mentioned selling her house. As the renter, should she not have talked to me about it first? I guess not.

**Melinda, my Mother**

What was Melinda up to? Where were Bud, Jeffrey, and I supposed to live? I had rented my mother's home for over four years and took diligent care of the house. I did all the upkeep and maintenance. I took care of the pool and paid all the bills related to the house.

Later, I found out a realtor had convinced my mother to sell her house. He showed her the substantial equity she had gained while she owned the house. Melinda saw dollar signs.

The other issue that influenced Melinda to sell her house was that she did not like the person I was dating, Renea. After two failed marriages, fraught with mental and physical abuse, I ceased all relationships with men. It was my contention to not have any relationship and focus on raising Bud and Jeffrey.

However, a situation came up when I met Renea, as it reminded me at the age of ten, I experienced an attraction for women. At that time, where I grew up, this was not an option. My father had a gay brother, and he despised him. I also had a gay relative in California. For my parents, first, it was not their child, and second, she lived in California, which explained everything to Melinda and Torrance.

## Discussion

However, before I pursued this interest, I sat down with Bud and Jeffrey and shared a long talk with them. Bud was thirteen, and Jeffrey was ten. It was important to me that they understood what I thought and felt.

"I want to tell both of you what I am thinking. I refuse to live a lie. Do either of you have any questions?" I asked.

Bud replied, "Don't do anything weird in front of my friends. I don't want people thinking I'm gay."

"Yea, what Bud said." Jeffrey agreed.

"Thanks, I want both of you to understand it is not okay to lie. Things go better if you tell the truth. I love you both and would not do anything to hurt you."

"Love you too!" Jeffrey said.

"It would be nice if you were happy," Bud said.

## Mother's Spite

The biggest mistake I made was telling my mother. She was selfish and loved to control people. Melinda believed Renea would not be interested in me if I did not have a lovely pool home to entertain her in. So, Melinda sold her home.

When that did not get rid of Renea, Melinda called Bud and Jeffrey's father, Artie. She told him who I was dating and told him to take my children away from me. She claimed I was an unfit mother by dating a woman. That plan backfired on her. Artie still had no interest in being a parent to Bud and Jeffrey.

Jeffrey took great offense to his grandmother's behavior.

He said, "Mom, I got on my bicycle, rode over to Great Granddad's house, and rang the doorbell. When Grandma Melinda answered, I said, 'Grandma, I love my mother. I want to live with her. Never try to have me taken away from her again. Thank you.' I left and rode my bike home."

Jeffrey was more mature and rational than my own mother.

**Torrance, my Father**

Melinda took one last stab at hurting me though. She called my father Torrance, her ex-husband. She told him the story. She got satisfaction there. He called me and disowned me. I was twenty-nine years old.

Torrance said, "You are no longer my daughter."

"Thanks, I never thought you were my father to begin with," I responded.

**Leaving Bighorn**

After my mother's house sold and the school year ended, I bought a house in Fallen Meadow, Utah. Bud, Jeffrey, and I disappeared from our family. The Three Musketeers were on a new adventure.

To ensure that my family could not find us, I rented a mailbox in one of those mail places in a shopping mall. The mail store had an actual street address, not just a P.O. box address.

The things my family did to me—especially my mother—broke my heart, but this was not the first, nor would it be the last time they hurt me.

*Author's note:* Melinda gambled away all the money she made from the sale of her home. She ended up destitute and homeless. She lived with her children until her death.

CHAPTER 18

# MY MOTHER'S WORDS

The most horrific wound Melinda ever gave me happened that fateful night, March 28, 2001, when I found out somebody murdered Jeffrey. When Lynette met me at the distribution center in Fallen Meadow, she realized we should call our mother.

Melinda lived in Hooterville, Utah, a suburb of Fallen Meadow. She would have seen the local news stories, and the *Secret Witness* program requesting information about an eighteen-year-old murdered in a robbery. We knew the police had released Jeffrey's name after they completed the notification of the next of kin, naming Jeffrey as the victim of a violent crime.

Lynette said, "You'd better tell mom it was Jeffrey who was killed before she hears it on the television."

My mind could not even put that all together, but she dialed Melinda's number and handed me the phone. It was now March 29, 2001, at 2 a.m. The phone rang and rang. Finally, my mom answered.

"Why are you calling so late?" Melinda growled.

My brain swirled: What would this news do to my mother? She was not in the best of health, as she had recently survived heart surgery. Would I kill my mother with this horrifying news?

"Mom, Jeffrey has been murdered."

Melinda replied, "I know; I saw it on the news. Are you coming to Vegas? I need some money."

Her reply took a second to register in my traumatized brain. "Are you out of your freaking mind? Somebody murdered my son—your grandson, Jeffrey. You want f**king money? Have you no soul?"

I handed the phone to Lynette. I have no idea if she talked to our mother or not. I almost threw up on the spot, as I tasted the bitter, angry bile in my mouth.

How could my mother not know that I needed her more, at that very instant, than I ever needed her in my entire life? She expressed zero empathy for me and not an ounce of sympathy.

I did not speak to her again for two years and five months. Yes, I know the exact date, the exact time. It was all about Melinda, as usual. I not only lost my baby, Jeffrey, that night on March 28, 2001, but I also lost my mother too.

CHAPTER 19

# THE DOWNWARD SLIDE

June of 1994 brought more changes in the lives of the Three Musketeers. Working my ass off as a local delivery driver for Box Trucking in Fallen Meadow, Utah, earned me a promotion to Turquoise, Arizona. No more loading and unloading hundreds of trailers for this girl.

On this new job, I drove from terminal to terminal and slept in a hotel room. I was an elite line driver now. Little did I realize that being the only female truck driver to ever work at Box Trucking in Turquoise did not sit well with over a hundred male drivers. Yep, the harassment started at once.

Two things happened with the move. First, Bud decided to live with his father, Artie, in Wisconsin. The move would be a good change for Jeffrey and me, I thought. However, I needed a babysitter for Jeffrey when I worked out of town.

Second, I have no idea what I was thinking. I must have lost my mind, but I invited Melinda to move to Turquoise, Arizona with us. She had just retired from J Davis & Co. and was tired of living with her father in Bighorn, Utah.

Why did I never learn?

## A New Home

Things went well for a while. Melinda looked at homes I might be interested in buying while I worked. I bought the last one she ever imagined I would buy. It was a double-wide modular home on an acre of land. Melinda quickly named it, *Belly Acre Ranch*!

Jeffrey and I refurbished the inside. Wyatt, and his family came up from Salt River, Arizona and helped Jeffrey, Melinda, and me fence and cross fence the acre. Then they built a chicken coop. I paid all the bills.

## Funny Melinda Story

Melinda and I went down to the Farm Store to get chicks for the newly built chicken coop. At the store, an innocent looking young man, high school age, possible first job, came to help my mother.

"Hello, my name is Finn, may I help you Ma'am?"

"Yes, I'd like twenty-eight female chicks please." Melinda said proudly.

Finn looked worried and said, "I don't know how to tell the boy chicks from the girl chicks ma'am, I'll get the manager."

"Oh, it's easy to tell Finn." Melinda replied. "The boy chicks say, 'cock-a-doodle-doo,' and the girl chicks say, 'any-cock-will-do,' that's how you tell."

I about fainted. I had no idea my mother would say such a thing. She must have waited years to throw that joke out, just at the right time. Finn turned about six shades of red. He was speechless; hell, I was speechless too.

"Mom, really, was that necessary?"

"Kathy, it's just a joke." Melinda laughed.

Thankfully, it was 1994, and people were not *politically correct* all the time. We all took a breath and laughed. I am sure that Finn never forgot that day at the Farm Store. Funny thing, Melinda bought twenty-eight girl chickens. I still was not sure how Finn figured it out, but he got it correct.

**More Family Members**

Next thing I knew, Renea, the first woman I dated—whom my mother sold her house over—also moved to Turquoise. I had no idea why. Could my life get any better?

We were still friends, or so I thought. One night, Renea called and wanted to introduce me to this other woman, Kori, who was single. Next thing I knew, Kori was my—non-working, useless girlfriend—and living with us.

Bud's adventure with his father did not work out. He returned home after his freshman year in high school. It was nice to have Bud back, but he was not happy being in Turquoise, Arizona. The school was boring. He complained they were not teaching him anything.

**School System Disasters**

The public-school system in Arizona was no more prepared for Jeffrey's learning disabilities than Utah had been. We thought things would improve when Jeffrey entered the eighth grade. The school was all excited about a new program they were implementing. Jeffrey would be in a small class with a four-to-one teacher ratio in a special program for at-risk children with learning disabilities.

Unfortunately, this program did not develop as planned. They had an innovative idea, but they never implemented their plan. Jeffrey's teacher sent him home when they did not want to deal with him. After they sent Jeffrey home for the twentieth time, the school called me. Mind you, there were no earlier notifications of this being a problem.

"Do not send Jeffrey back to school," they said.

"What is he supposed to do for school?" I asked.

"He will be promoted to high school in August," they said.

"So, what am I supposed to do with him until August?" I asked.

"That is up to you; he will go to high school in August."

This was unacceptable to me, but as a single parent, I had to continue to work, so Jeffrey stayed home for the week, supposedly supervised by Melinda and Kori. It took me a little time to figure this out.

## Another Nightmare

Unbelievably, while I was at work, Jeffrey came home with two *real* tattoos. Yes, you read that correctly—*real* tattoos. I do not know who, or why, but somebody gave a fourteen-year-old boy real tattoos. Yes, this was totally illegal.

Jeffrey would not tell me, or the police, who gave him the tattoos. I can honestly say I lost my mind at that point. Jeffrey had extremely inappropriate, permanent tattoos on his arms. There were no words to describe the anger and disappointment I felt. With nothing else I could do until morning, I cried.

The next morning, I took Jeffrey to a doctor in Turquoise, Arizona.

He said, "I could try to take the tattoos off, but it would cost a thousand dollars an inch to *try* to remove them. There is no guarantee it would work."

"Are you kidding me?" I asked. "There is nothing else you can do?"

"I suggest you have the tattoos covered-up with professional tattoos," he said.

There appeared to be no better solution. I could not afford a thousand dollars an inch to *try*. I needed a guaranteed fix. I took Jeffrey to Fallen Meadow, Utah. I found a professional tattoo artist and explained the situation. He agreed to fix them.

The tattoo on the back of Jeffrey's left upper arm was the words *Fuck It* in one-inch gothic letters shown in the first photo below.

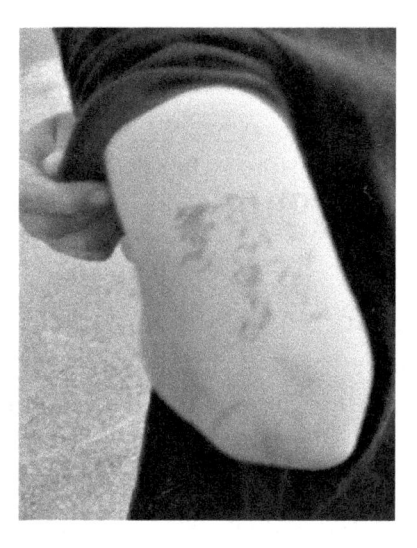

*F\*\*k It Tattoo*

This photo below showed the dragon head that covered it up.

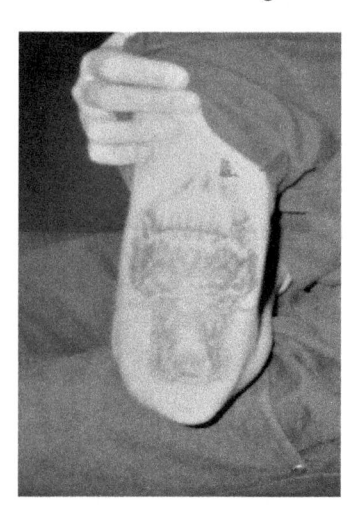

*Tattoo Cover Up*

The tattoo on Jeffrey's other arm was of a big-breasted, naked woman. The tattoo went from his wrist area to the crease of his elbow. Unbelievable. Either I was too shocked to take a photo, or I lost the photo in the shuffle.

*Naked Woman Cover Up*

However, the photo shows the covered-up tattoo. The tattoo artist put a colorful blue, full-bodied dragon over the big-breasted, naked woman. It turned out nicely, as far as tattoos on fourteen-year-old boys go.

The tattoo artist could not believe that anybody would do that to a fourteen-year-old boy.

"Jeffrey, who did the work?" he asked.

"I am not getting anybody in trouble," Jeffrey answered.

Jeffrey never revealed to me, or anyone I know of, who put the original tattoos on him. He was six-foot tall and weighed 180 pounds. Now, with professional tattoos, Jeffrey could walk into any tattoo shop in the country and get more tattoos without showing any identification card. Yes, he got more tattoos—fifteen in total.

## Things Escalated

A man jumped on Jeffrey's back during an altercation in a parking lot, causing Jeffrey to collapse to the ground. Of course, I was at work; I was always at work. After a three-day run to California, when I arrived at the Box Trucking terminal, the dispatcher gave me the following message.

"Your son Josh is in the emergency room with a broken arm."

"I do not have a son named Josh."

"Well, something like that; go to the emergency room."

When I got to the hospital, I found out that the incident caused Jeffrey's leg to break in four places. That was bad enough, but the bones slid off the growth plate in his foot. This injury required surgery to place the bones back on his growth plate and fix the broken bones.

Jeffrey would need X-rays on his leg monthly to make sure the bones reattached to the growth plate and were growing. If the bones had not grown, they would have had to stop the other leg from growing. Thankfully, the surgery worked. His leg continued to grow as he matured, and he grew to six foot, three inches tall.

## Huffing Spray Paint?

Things continued to spiral for Jeffrey. The final straw happened when the police picked him up and brought him home. For once, I was home.

They said, "We think he was huffing spray paint.

"What does that mean?"

"Huffing spray paint is when a person fills a paper bag with the contents of a can of spray paint. With the bag full of paint fumes, they put the bag over their mouth and nose area, and then they inhale the contents of the bag. The paint could coat the lungs and cause instant death."

"Why would Jeffrey do such a dumb thing?" I asked aloud.

"Huffing seems to be a phase that kids think is fun."

The whole thing was asinine. I was beyond fed up with Jeffrey's behavior. What the hell was going on with this boy?

CHAPTER 20

# THE END OF MY ROPE

Jeffrey's acting out propelled me to take a hard look at my life. I was extremely exhausted. I not only supported my two sons, but I also had a non-working girlfriend and my mother living in my house.

The hours I spent driving a truck down the highways of America had these thoughts swirling through my brain: How had everything gone so wrong? When I first moved to Turquoise, I thought things would be good. Jeffrey had a fresh start at a new school. It was a small town, like Pluto, Illinois, the town I grew up in. I imagined Jeffrey having friends, playing sports, and enjoying his teenage years. I always wanted my sons to have the childhood I never had.

Every time I left for work, I felt like I had the weight of the world on my shoulders. They all lined up at the door with their hands out, expecting to receive, at minimum, a $20 bill. Melinda found the situation hilarious, but she always got in line for her $20.

How was I ever going to help Jeffrey, while continuing to support this hoard of ungrateful people? I was hanging onto the knot at the end of my rope and needed things to change quickly. Fed-up and depleted of any answers, I took a week off work.

**Answers Needed**

Jeffrey and I got in the car, and the two of us went to Fallen Meadow, Utah. He had no idea where he was going until I pulled into the psychiatric hospital my doctor recommended. They admitted Jeffrey for an evaluation. Previously, I warned Bud and Jeffrey of the higher risk factors they would confront about addiction, thanks to our family.

My father's parents were alcoholics and died of complications from it. Melinda's gambling addictions were out of control. I was a recovering alcoholic myself. Well, at least I had not had a drink in three years. So, it was better to snip the addiction bug, or the huffing thing in the bud.

Jeffrey was not happy, but I really did not care. I needed answers. After checking him into the psychiatric hospital, I left.

**Now What**

Not in my best state of mind, I drove straight to my favorite bar in Fallen Meadow. I parked my car, sat there alone, and cried. I was under so much stress.

Fatigued from working irregular hours on a seniority board at this job with men who did not want me there to begin with had exhausted me. They taught me more about sexual harassment and misogynistic behavior than I ever could have imagined.

The confusion of Jeffrey's behavior added to that reality, and I found myself extremely disillusioned with being a single parent. With no regard to my sobriety, there were two thoughts on my mind: I could get rip-roaring drunk, or I could kill myself. Even better, I could do both.

It had been three years since I had taken my last drink. I was what they called a dry drunk. I did not work the Alcoholics Anonymous twelve-step program. I just did not take a drink. Those meetings worked for other people; obviously, they had no idea who I was.

I honestly believed the program would never work for me. I was beyond help. I carried copious amounts of baggage from my childhood and earlier marriages. That program had no idea the hell I had survived and dealt with in my head.

## Make That Call

Before I walked into that bar, the memory that I was supposed to call somebody before taking that first drink came into my mind. Lynn, the office manager at Box Trucking in Fallen Meadow, popped into my head. I knew she was in the AA Program, so I called her. Surprisingly, she answered.

"Lynn, this is Kathy, I am about to go into a bar and give up three years of sobriety. Or I am going to kill myself."

Whatever. I would be able to say I called somebody before I took that first drink. I always liked to follow the rules to the extent that they made me look good.

"Kathy, give me one year and do everything exactly as I tell you to do, no questions asked. At the end of that year, if you still want to kill yourself, I won't stop you."

Deep down, I guess I really did not want to kill myself or take that first drink. "I'm so very tired of being everything and taking care of everyone. Nobody ever takes care of me. I guess I can try it, but if it does not work, I am not going to play any longer. I will kill myself. I cannot take it anymore."

"Deal!" Lynn said.

Never in my wildest dreams could I ever imagine the storm over the horizon in my life.

## CHAPTER 21
# ATTITUDE ADJUSTMENT

Jeffrey spent a couple of weeks at the psychiatric hospital. They ran dozens of tests, and Jeffrey spoke with medical doctors and psychiatrists. He also attended group therapies. We shared no communications for the week, which was strange for us, as we always talked to each other. The doctor called me at the end of the two-week period with his conclusions.

"There are no indications of mental illness," the psychiatrist said.

"Well, that is a good thing, correct?"

"Jeffrey needs an attitude adjustment. I suggest you send Jeffrey to Raging Waters Treatment Program in Potato, Utah."

I am a good parent, so I followed the doctor's orders. However, my insurance company did not cover the program their psychiatrist recommended. This made me angry, and I got into an argument with the insurance person on the phone.

I demanded, "Why would your company pay $1000 a day for the psychiatric hospital, but when your doctor recommends that Jeffrey be placed in this wilderness treatment center, you will not pay for it?"

"That program is not covered."

"Who gets the kickback on the psychiatric hospital?" I asked.

She hung up on me.

## Wilderness Treatment Program

I decided to put Jeffrey in the program, as he needed help. Bud went with me to pick Jeffrey up at the hospital and take him to the Wilderness Treatment Program. We shared a nice dinner and explained the program to Jeffrey. There was no problem with Jeffrey attending.

He said, "Whatever you want me to do, Mom."

*Bud (17) and Jeffrey (14)*

The children in this program had supervision twenty-four hours a day, and they saw a psychiatrist weekly. There was no reason insurance could not pay for this treatment. It was less expensive than the psychiatric hospital. The whole thing was suspicious to me.

For seventy-four days, I did not see or talk to Jeffrey. He lived in the wilderness and mountains of southern Utah. The program forced him to earn everything he received, including food. Jeffrey later described it as being on the television show *Survivor*, without a chance to win a million dollars.

The staff called me one time during the seventy-four days to tell me they took Jeffrey to the hospital. He was extremely sick—throwing up, fever, and weakness. They diagnosed him with giardiasis from drinking bad water. When Jeffrey returned to the program, the counselor called and reported he was okay.

Upon release, they invited me to stay one night on the mountain with Jeffrey. He took care of me, including cooking our meal and securing our place to sleep. It was quite a change from me having to be the one who had taken care of everybody.

"Mom, when they took me to the hospital, they put a bag over my head."

This shocked me. I had no idea about the treatment that he received. "Are you kidding me?"

"Nope, they said the bag kept me from knowing where I was or what hospital they took me to."

I confirmed with the staff later.

"Yes, it stops escapes."

Had I known the truth; I might not have placed Jeffrey there. *Hindsight is 20/20!*

Jeffrey changed greatly. First, he lost fifty pounds. He appeared free of any adverse effects from the huffed spray paint. He survived in the wilderness and gained survival skills for any disaster. Unfortunately, deep acne infected his face from lack of cleanliness.

**Boarding School**

The psychiatrist recommended I send Jeffrey to Irish Hills, a boarding school for at-risk boys in Plateau, Washington. He thought the curriculum and supervision supplied would help Jeffrey continue the progress he made at the Wilderness Treatment Center and get Jeffrey caught up to his proper level in school, which would be 9th grade, or a freshman in high school.

I tried to do whatever I could to save my child. I made a promise to this child when I found out about his learning disabilities. I truly do not know if I blamed myself subconsciously for those disabilities, but I would live up to and fulfill that promise. I sacrificed everything to make a better life for my sons. It would be worth it, even if it cost me my sanity, my financial security, and my personal happiness.

The staff did not know the exact number of grade levels Jeffrey was behind but believed this at-risk boarding school could get Jeffrey caught up quickly. Again, I did what the medical professionals suggested. The boarding school had licensed counselors and therapists that lived with the boys. They also supplied a psychiatrist who visited each boy monthly and put them through a detailed evaluation.

Once again, my insurance would not cover the cost. This school was $3000 a month. Just after he arrived, Jeffrey and another boy ran away from the school. They found them on a Native American Reservation in Idaho. People quickly reported two young white boys. The police returned them to the school in Washington. That was the only negative behavioral incident while Jeffrey was at this school.

**My Struggles**

My life changed completely in 1996 from any picture I ever had of it. Alone, with neither of my children, all I did was work, sleep, worry, and repeat. Bud was at basic training for the U.S. Navy. I could not talk to him until his graduation in February. Jeffrey was at boarding school. I could talk to him for a brief time every Sunday. This would be the first time we were not together for the holidays.

Divided, the Three Musketeers still stood, but I was the one who struggled the most. I was even more alone after I cleaned out my house. I sent Melinda back to her father's house in Bighorn, Utah, and my ex-girlfriend back to Fallen Meadow.

I sold my house in Turquoise, and when I was not driving a big truck, I stayed with my friend Roger. I needed a vacation. I thought, *Why not?* I was already drowning in debt. What was a little more debt going to do, kill me? I could only be so lucky.

**Vacation and Funny Jeffrey Story**

For Christmas, Jeffrey and I flew to the island of Tahiti. From the airport, we took a bus to a boat. The boat took us to the island of Moorea. We stayed there for a week.

Here's a funny story about Jeffrey's trip to the Tahitian Islands, which are part of French Polynesia. When we started our trip, Jeffrey thought it weird that I always said "Hello" or "Good Morning" to the people I passed.

"Mom, you don't have to talk to everybody. You're like Grandma Melinda."

"Whatever Jeffrey, I'm just being polite."

It was late when we got to the island and checked into the hotel. The next morning, we went down for what they called our complimentary American breakfast, included in our package. As we ate breakfast at the beachfront restaurant, Jeffrey looked out the window onto the beach and at the beautiful water.

Jeffrey suddenly realized the women sunbathing did not have the tops of their swimsuits on. He could not believe his eyes. Things looked up quickly for a fifteen-year-old boy going through puberty at an all-boys boarding school.

After breakfast, we walked out to the beach. Jeffrey stared at all the girls, just a little bit too low. He smiled and said, "Good morning!"

"Jeffrey, look about ten inches higher when you say *Good morning*, and it will mean a whole lot more to the ladies."

Sharing this precious time with him allowed me to see the changes that had taken place while he was away at school and the growth he experienced at Irish Hills. Jeffrey took a scuba diving lesson. We went on a shark-feeding boat trip and snorkeling. The scary part was that Jeffrey could hold his breath for about four minutes. He went underwater, and it scared me half to death when he did not come back up.

We rented a scooter and took a ride around the island. There was only one road on the island, so I let Jeffrey drive us. Believe me, it was quite an adventure. We rode around the island and looked at the hurricane damage from the storm earlier that summer.

**Back to School**

We enjoyed a great vacation. We flew back to Poison Oak, California, then on to Plateau, Washington, and Jeffrey went back to school. I flew home to Fallen Meadow, Utah, and went back to work at Box Trucking in Turquoise, Arizona.

We were halfway through Jeffrey's time at boarding school. Things were going well for him. He was turning into a nice young man. The year at boarding school created changes we had not expected, and we learned things that helped Jeffrey get through the rest of his education.

The most important thing we learned was if Jeffrey read something, it made no sense to him. However, if he read the information and discussed it with somebody, he understood the information. With this technique, he received straight As in school.

Jeffrey also learned how to dance. There was free time on the weekends, so the boys taught each other how to dance. As a girl who attended junior high and high school dances where the boys seldom danced, I told both Bud and Jeffrey that girls loved the boys who could dance and asked the girls to dance. Jeffrey believed me, as he sure could dance.

## The Boy Becomes a Man

Jeffrey's voice changed when he went through puberty. One Sunday, I called and asked for Jeffrey.

He said, "This is Jeff."

The person's voice was the deepest, manly, movie-star-like voice I had ever heard. "No, I wanted little Jeff."

"Mom, this is Jeff," he replied.

"Jeffrey, what the hell happened?" I asked.

"I don't know. I just woke up, and this is what my voice sounded like. Cool, huh?"

It was so nice to hear Jeffrey laugh. He was excited and thought it fun.

"Wait until you hear me sing songs," Jeffrey said.

After Jeffrey's voice changed, girls asked him questions, just to hear him talk. He thought it was funny, but he cooperated with the girls and answered their questions.

## Spring Break

I planned a trip to Hawaii. Melinda—still on good behavior—Jeffrey, and I took off for the Islands of Hawaii. Jeffrey and I were very much alike and always up for an adventure, so we decided to go parasailing.

What a blast! We laughed, talked, and enjoyed the scenery. The boat driver even dipped us in the water a couple of times. It was a wonderful spring break. Jeffrey had grown and matured at boarding school. He was thrilled to have a break in Hawaii. We both loved the islands, and we even brough Melinda along.

*Jeffrey at a Luau*

Jeffrey went back to school. He only had three more months, and he would finish at the boarding school. It was an exceptionally long year without Jeffrey. It would be fun to learn all the things he experienced during this year and a half away from home. He had met people from all over the country. He would have stories to tell. He was a delightful storyteller.

I looked forward to spending the summer with him. I would have a chance to see if he really had changed. Think back to your childhood days and remember how you could not wait for the last day of school and summer vacation. Jeffrey and I were doubly excited, as he would get out of school for the summer, and he got to come home. The school fulfilled its promises to Jeffrey and me, as he finished his freshmen year in high school, caught up to his grade level.

Jeffrey was excited when I told him we were moving to Florida before school started. It would be a new beginning for him and a new adventure for both of us. I made a surprise plan for Jeffrey and me to spend the summer traveling around the United States. It would give him a chance to see more of America. Jeffrey and I were free for the summer.

## CHAPTER 22

# SUMMER VACATION

Since the company I worked for, Box Trucking, would not allow people to ride along with me in the truck, I quit. My priorities were different than theirs. My promise was to get Jeffrey through high school, and that was what I would do. My purpose in life was to raise my two sons, whatever it took.

Besides, I would not miss the harassment I received at this job. This job was one of the most challenging I ever had. Not that the job was difficult, but the men were not happy to have me there at all. They made it truly clear they thought I should go home and give my job to a man.

They said, "You should be home, naked, serving dinner to a man."

At half a dozen terminals I delivered to, there was only a men's restroom with no door. They refused to put a door on the restroom.

They said, "If she wants to be a man, she can piss like a man. We are not putting a door on the restroom."

Another thing they did was mess with my truck and trailer. When I hooked my tractor-trailer up to leave the terminal, I had to go in and clock out. When I came back out, I had to re-check everything, as they would disconnect things. Then they waited to laugh at me. It was incredibly stressful. I could have won lawsuits, if only I filed them. The harassment was ridiculous.

They laughed when I said I was quitting my job. They scoffed at me and said, "Nobody quits this job." How surprised they were when I quit showing up for work and their harassment.

I found a driving job with a company out of Potato, Utah. This company allowed Jeffrey to ride along in the truck with me for the summer. We traveled wherever the trucking company sent us; it was a blast. When our trailer emptied, I asked for a load to somewhere we had never been before, so Jeffrey could see somewhere new and exciting.

Jeffrey and I traveled through thirty-six states in less than three months. He kept track of each state as we went through them on a big laminated map I carried in my truck. This was way before GPS and cell phones.

We spent the 4$^{th}$ of July at a truck stop in Wyoming and watched the most beautiful fireworks. The night sky was so clear and full of stars. We could see forever, and it made the fireworks spectacular. Jeffrey and I enjoyed watching them from the cab of my truck.

**Jeffrey Meets Artie**

One night, Jeffrey and I stopped at a truck stop in Sicily, Wisconsin, for the night. I shared the story of his birth and how we ended up in this town's hospital when he was born. Jeffrey looked at his map book and realized we were near his father's home. Curious, he asked if he could call his father.

How sad that a fifteen-year-old boy had to ask to meet his father for the first time in his memory.

Jeffrey said, "I would like to meet him and introduce myself. I don't even remember what he looks like."

I gave Jeffrey the phone number and he called. I could not tell if Jeffrey was nervous or not, but he was determined for sure. His father Artie answered, I was sure he was surprised to find out it was Jeffrey on the phone. Jeffrey introduced himself and explained where we were.

Jeffrey asked, "Would you and your wife like to meet us for dinner at the truck stop?"

Surprisingly, they agreed to drive up to Sicily. It was only forty-eight miles from the farm. While we waited, Jeffrey and I showered and dressed for dinner at the truck stop. When traveling in a tractor-trailer, one did not have fancy clothes, as Jeffrey called them, but we cleaned up as best we could.

Artie and Gail arrived and shared dinner with us. Jeffrey had recently celebrated his fifteenth birthday. Artie did not remember Jeffrey's birthday.

How sad. It was an uncomfortable moment, but Jeffrey kept the conversation flowing and asked questions of his father.

Jeffrey asked about farming and cattle. He also asked about family members he did not know. I was proud of Jeffrey. He used his manners and acted mature. He had become an adult.

I made polite conversation as I really had nothing to say to either one of them. These two people destroyed my marriage and took their father from my children. Artie stepped up and paid the bill. Impressive, since he owed me thousands of dollars in back child support.

Artie asked, "May we look at the tractor-trailer?"

Jeffrey gave them the ten-cent-tour, as my granddad used to call it. They thanked us for our time. Jeffrey and Artie shook hands and they left. Jeffrey was quiet, processing his life and his father.

The only other time Jeffrey had seen his father was when Jeffrey was six years old. Grandmother Reba, diagnosed with terminal cancer, wanted to see her two grandsons before she died. She asked me if the boys could visit her. Bud and Jeffrey flew to see her and say their goodbyes. So, from the age of eight-months-old to his death, Jeffrey saw his father twice.

Jeffrey and I finished our summer of traveling around the country. We took the tractor-trailer back to Potato, Utah, and turned it in. I was still in my mother's good graces, so she drove down from Fallen Meadow and picked us up.

## CHAPTER 23

# PEACE AND HAPPINESS

Wow! Finally, we were back together as a family—Bud, Jeffrey, and me. The Three Musketeers. So much had changed in our lives. Jeffrey was so excited to see Bud again. It had been such a long, harrowing, and expensive road, but the three of us found peace in Florida. We loved the warm weather and all the water, especially the Atlantic Ocean.

The biggest surprise to Jeffrey was that Bud got married. Bud and Jodi lived in a cute house near the Navy base. It was only a two-bedroom house with one bathroom, but they offered to let Jeffrey and I stay with them.

We stayed for two months while I found a job and a place for us to live. Jeffrey and I shared a bedroom, which was quite an adventure for both of us. Thankfully, I had kept the boys' bunk beds when we moved, as Jeffrey and I shared a room. He got the top bunk, so I was not climbing up and down all the time.

**Life's a Beach**

Jeffrey and I decided we wanted to live by the beach on the Atlantic Ocean. So, I started to look for rentals out at Cowford Beach, Florida. I found a cute little duplex to rent three blocks from the Atlantic Ocean with a beautiful sandy beach and gorgeous sunrises. Jeffrey and I loved living by the ocean; it was so peaceful.

This was a different lifestyle from the desert we had lived in for years. The beach had a very laid-back atmosphere. Jeffrey and I both enjoyed living in a beach community. I ran on the beach every morning for three miles. Fit and trim, I felt healthy, at peace, and happy. It was nice to find serenity for once.

I attended a couple of Alcoholics Anonymous meetings in Cowford, Florida. I met a lady who recommended a job that serviced car dealerships. It worked out perfectly, as they needed somebody at the beach area.

The Navy base was on the other side of Cowford from the beach, about fifteen miles away. When Bud and his Navy friends got off work, he called and got a wave condition report. Jeffrey or I walked down to the beach and checked the wave heights.

If the wave conditions were good, Bud and his Navy friends would drive out to the beach. They parked in my driveway, as parking at the beach was horrible. The boys would surf for hours. When they finished surfing, they came back to the house, and I fixed them food. Bud was always hungry, especially after surfing.

The Three Musketeers were a family again. It was such an enjoyable time. We spent time together with the Navy boys and listened to their stories of the waves and work. Bud and Jeffrey both loved surfing. I did not surf, but I enjoyed watching them all surf. The Navy boys were away from home, and we became a family of sorts for them with home cooking and hanging out together.

**Jeffrey Matures**

Jeffrey also loved to skateboard. He was an amazing athlete and could jump all kinds of things, flip his board, and land on it. Watching Jeffrey skateboard used to scare me half to death. He never broke anything besides the boards, thankfully. I bought him nine different skateboards during the two years we lived in Cowford Beach, Florida. He amazed me.

After we settled in at the beach, Jeffrey got a job, as he wanted to make his own spending money. His first job was at the local car wash. He enjoyed that until summer set in. It became hot and humid in Florida during the summer.

I had given Bud a 1969 Nova when he joined the Navy, so I gave Jeffrey a car for his sixteenth birthday. It was a 1993 Geo Prizm. The rule was Jeffrey paid for gas, insurance, and upkeep, or no car.

Jeffrey's second job was at an Italian Restaurant on the beach where he washed dishes instead. "Mom, the restaurant job is better than the car wash. They have air conditioning, and I get to eat for free."

"Geez Jeffrey, you sound like Bud," I said.

**Driver's License**

Jeffrey got his driver's license, but when I went to give him the car, I realized he did not know how to drive a five-speed stick shift vehicle. I took him to an abandoned shopping center parking lot and taught him the skill of easing the clutch and applying the gas at the same time.

Patience was not my middle name, as the car lurched and stalled. Start, lurch, stall, and repeat. My mind raced with thoughts of *why?* Why had I not thought to buy him an automatic shifting car? Why did I always try to do the correct thing, but screw it up? Why did I always try to fix the world for everybody?

I could laugh or I could cry. Memories of my childhood flooded back as I recalled that when I learned to drive, my parents were going through a horrific divorce, and court battles ensued. I made sure my children had the childhood that I never had, so I took a deep breath and taught Jeffrey to drive.

He got frustrated at first, as was common for him with his learning disabilities. Hell, that was common for anyone learning to drive a stick shift vehicle. Thankfully, he quickly got the hang of it. After an hour of practice, I allowed him to drive me home. Lucky for us, Florida did not have hills, so the process was easier to learn.

Jeffrey continued his *f*ck it* attitudes (remember the tattoo). He mostly wore this hat backward. It became a fixture on his head. However, he always took it off his head at my request, especially at the table for dinner.

*Jeffrey's F**k It Hat*

Jeffrey attended public high school while we lived at the beach, which was a financial break for me. He did okay. He kept up with his schoolwork, which was a challenge, but we worked together until high school graduation was in sight.

Bud, Jeffrey, and I spent time together whenever we could. Jodi worked on Saturdays, so Bud came out to the beach and spent time with us. We ate breakfast and went to the laundromat since I had to do laundry on my day off work. We talked about work and life.

Bud said, "Mom, this is the first time I have ever seen you at peace. You are so relaxed and happy here at the beach in Florida. You should always live by water. We have each other, and life is good. Together, the Three Musketeers have grown up and come so far."

Jeffrey agreed, "Yea Mom, we are back as a family. I love you!"

"I love both of you more than you will ever know!"

"Oh Mom, we know!" Bud said.

In the evening, Bud and Jeffrey went out with the Navy guys. In Florida, the age to go to the dance clubs was eighteen. Even though Jeffrey was sixteen, he walked right into the clubs. Bud got his ID checked every time they went in. It made him so mad. Jeffrey danced the night away with the girls. Bud and his friends were frustrated when Jeffrey had a dozen girls dancing with him. Jeffrey loved it.

**New Adventures**

One day, Chad, a friend and ex-coworker from Box Trucking in Turquoise, called me unexpectedly.

He asked, "Would Jeffrey be interested in learning how to scuba dive? I need somebody to dive with, and I would be willing to pay for his lessons if he were interested."

I said, "I'm sure he would; he loves the water. I'll ask him."

Of course, Jeffrey jumped right on the offer and passed the course with no problems. Chad flew to Florida for dive trips all around the state. They went cave diving at Devil's Den and Blue Grotto in Williston, Florida, and boat diving off both coasts of Florida. I became a certified diver when we lived in Hawaii in 1986 and was able to join them. Later, Chad called with another offer.

Chad asked, "Would you and Jeffery like to go on a dive trip to the Grand Cayman Islands with me? I will purchase the tickets."

We both agreed to go. Without Chad's generosity, we would never have been able to afford such a luxurious trip. The island and water were beautiful; it was a wonderful trip that we never forgot.

*Jeffrey Scuba Diving Grand Cayman*

This photo shows Jeffrey and his adventurous personality. He dove with the stingrays and piranhas. He had absolutely no fear of being one hundred feet underwater, or with biting fish. He never wanted to go home. The trip with Chad was a wonderful time for both Jeffrey and me. I am quite sure Chad enjoyed it too.

Jeffrey loved every minute diving. He was like a fish in the water. We spent five days and did fifteen dives, including a couple of night dives. We went through caves and tunnels under forty feet of water. It was crazy; we used maps and flashlights to navigate. The water was so clear, and the fish were beautiful.

We toured the island and went to the town of Hell, Grand Cayman. We bought a postcard at a local store and mailed it to Melinda, which reflected the struggles Jeffrey and I had been through. The postcard shared these words.

*I've Been to Hell and Back.*

I said aloud, "Jeffrey is going to be okay. Somehow, we survived his disabilities, the public-school systems, and his juvenile struggles."

## Graduation

Jeffrey finished high school. He graduated early by taking his last two courses online. What an accomplishment! He received his high school diploma from Front Range High School in Colorado. I had fulfilled my promise to that little five-year-old Jeffrey, all those years ago.

There was not a word big enough to describe what I felt for Jeffrey. He achieved a miracle. Bud, Jeffrey, and I enjoyed a huge celebration dinner. Jeffrey's diploma hangs on my wall, still today.

## Change in the Air

Unfortunately, things never stayed peaceful for long in my life. Bud, Jeffrey, and I finally found a home in Florida. Things were going well for all three of us. We enjoyed dozens of trips and just hung out together at the beach. It was the first time in our lives that we were content and happy.

I found a perfect quote that described my life. Winston Churchill paraphrased the quote.

*Those who fail to learn from history are condemned to repeat it.*

One would think I had learned my lessons, especially when it came to Melinda, but I did not. History repeated itself in my life where she was concerned.

She called me unexpectedly one day, and I made the mistake of answering the phone call.

"Kathy, I need to have open-heart surgery so they can replace a defective valve in my heart. They are going to put a cow's valve in to fix my heart murmur. They will not do the surgery if I don't have a place to go after the surgery. Can you come back to Utah and help me?"

How ironic. My mother had done so many mean things to me. Why would I feel obligated to help her at all? Melinda had two other children who both lived in the same town as our mother. In fact, they lived mere blocks away from her.

However, neither one of them would take her into their homes after her surgery, even for two weeks. She must have burned more bridges while I was in Florida. So, my mother expected me to move all the way across this country to help her. I should have hung up the phone.

I should have yelled, "Hell, no!"

Instead, I said, "Sure."

CHAPTER 24

# NOTHING LASTS FOREVER

Leaving Florida was not what I wanted or needed to do. There, I shared a life of love, fun, and companionship with my two sons. It was a time of joy in my life I had not previously experienced. My huge sense of responsibility got the better of me. Even after all that Melinda had done to me, after all the horrible ways she treated me, she was still my mother. She needed my help, and that took precedence.

Yes, Jeffrey and I would take care of her through surgery and recovery, but in my mind and heart, I knew we would return to Florida. This was where I found a sense of love and peace.

*One step forward and three steps back.*

**Moving Again**

Once again, I rented a U-Haul truck. Jeffrey, Bud, his Navy friends, and I loaded up our belongings. We put my Mustang car on a trailer behind the truck. Jeffrey followed behind in his Geo Prizm.

Melinda was glad to have us back to help her with her medical issues. She always picked a favorite child, and if you were the favorite, she was great. If you were not, all hell was available for her to use against you.

I heard my entire life the story of how she suffered so horribly in her childhood. Melinda told us how her mother played favorite's and her favorite was always Melinda's brother. According to Melinda, he got everything. Bud and Jeffrey could tell the story exactly as my mother did and in her tone of voice.

"In 1942, I wanted a Coke. Did I get a Coke? No, Mark got the Coke. He was our mother's favorite." She would say.

If my mother was so miserable under those circumstances, why did she choose to live her life the same way and treat her children, grandchildren, and great-grandchildren the exact same way as she had supposedly been treated? I never understood any of it; however, it made me a better parent. I never treated my children that way.

Anyway, I was back in Melinda's good graces, and she needed me. I was the favorite. For how long, who knew?

Bud stayed in Cowford, Florida, in the Navy at Blind Field until the end of 1999. After two and a half years of marriage, Bud and Jodi divorced. I never heard the story of why they broke up. Neither one of them ever confided in me what happened in their relationship.

Jodi remained in Florida. The Navy transferred Bud to Mattapony Naval Air Station in Mattaponi, Maryland, for the rest of his enlisted commitment.

**Police Harassment Began**

I thought Jeffrey graduating from high school would mean one less stressful thing to deal with. Even though he had graduated, he was only seventeen years old. To Jeffrey, this meant he was an adult; to the local police, it meant he was a juvenile. The local police harassed Jeffrey incessantly, as a juvenile out after curfew.

Bighorn, Utah, had a juvenile problem at least as far back as the 70s when I first moved there, if not before. Teenagers complained regularly there was nothing to do there. So, the local police took no positive notice of a seventeen-year-old who had achieved good things; instead, they called him a liar.

They did not believe he graduated from high school, even after I showed them his high school diploma. It meant nothing to them that Jeffrey had a diploma, nor that he graduated from high school at seventeen years of age.

The local police then decided to harass me. They told me I needed to report to them if Jeffrey was not at home at midnight. If I did not, they would come after me as an unfit parent. Having been a law enforcement officer in the 1980s in Fallen Meadow, I did not appreciate this harassment.

By this time, I was working for the Dutch Corporation out of Maine. I drove a dedicated run from Fallen Meadow, Utah, to Waterloo, Texas. I left on Sunday night and returned on Thursday. Melinda and Jeffrey stayed together when I was at work. If I was home, I set my alarm clock for 11:59 p.m., got up, and looked to see if Jeffrey was in his bed. If he was not, I called the police.

"Jeffrey is not home." I hung up.

Melinda did the same thing when I was at work. It was ridiculous. When Jeffrey left the house, he was always polite and loving. He always kissed us goodbye and exchanged the same conversation.

"I love you."

"I love you, too, Jeffrey."

"Do whatever you need to do with the police. I'll see you in the morning."

"Okay Jeffrey."

That scenario never changed. He was not disrespectful to his grandmother or me. In his mind, he was an adult.

## Harassment of Melinda

One night when I was at work, the police called the house. They demanded Melinda, just out of the hospital, drive to Fallen Meadow to pick Jeffrey up at Juvenile Hall. She called me. I was livid and called them at once. I asked to speak with the Sergeant.

"Your officers took Jeffrey into Fallen Meadow for nothing more than harassment. They can bring him back."

I made it clear to him that I was driving a tractor-trailer to Texas and back every week, and it was extremely unacceptable for his officers to call and threaten my mother, as she had just survived open-heart surgery. Not yet released to drive a car, I reminded him that if she were to drive a vehicle *on their orders* and caused an accident, it would be on his head.

He apologized, and they never called Melinda again. You would think things could not get worse, but they did. A week later she walked to the store to get a newspaper. A car pulled out of a fast food restaurant and hit her. Somebody called 911 for help.

The local police responded. However, they would not call for an ambulance. My injured mother needed to go to the emergency room, but the police knew she was Jeffrey's grandmother. Luckily, Jeffrey drove by and saw it was his grandmother on the ground. He stopped to see what happened. Thankfully, he got her into his car and took her to the hospital as she had broken her arm.

## Search and Seizure

The harassment continued. The local police believed Jeffrey sold drugs. However, they never found any drugs in Jeffrey's possession, nor proved that he sold them. They even showed up at the house with a search warrant. Melinda and I were home when the police knocked on the front door.

They searched inside and outside of the house. They found absolutely nothing. That was not enough harassment for one night though, as later that night, I caught the local police in the alley behind the house going through our trash cans. I called 911 and reported a burglary, as I had strangers in my back yard. The dispatcher laughed, as she already knew who it was.

It was at this time in 1999 that I met Kim. Melinda and Kim became best friends instantly. I found this odd after the way she treated Renea previously, but at least there was peace in the family on that front.

## The Final Harassment

How different things might have been if the police and community had invested their funding and time in programs to help teenagers, instead of ruining their lives.

The final Bighorn harassment:

1. The local police arrested Jeffrey for truancy.

2. They seized Jeffrey's Geo Prizm.

*The police cannot do that*, people say. Well, they can, and they did. Seizure laws are preposterous in the United States. I should have gotten an attorney, as it was an unlawful search and seizure.

I called the city attorney countless times and received no response. This was the only vehicle we owned at the time. Thankfully, Kim owned her vehicle. It took six months to obtain an appointment with the city attorney.

Kim went with me to see the city attorney. I explained to him that Jeffrey was in juvenile hall, and I needed the car to care for my mother. He could have cared less. He pulled out the impound report filed by the police.

"This report says the car has a $1500 stereo in it. When we have our forfeiture sale, we will sell it for at least $1500."

"The car is not worth $1500. It is a 1993 Geo Prizm with over 250,000 miles."

"If you want the car back, write us a check for $1500."

What else could I do? I paid the $1500 and got the car back.

# CHAPTER 25

# THE SOUL TRAIN ROLLING

*Death #1* was my ninety-seven-year-old Grandfather Adam, who died in August of 2000. *All Aboard!* The red lights flashed, and the gates crashed down as the *Soul Train* roared into town. Melinda, Kim, and I continued to stay in his home in Bighorn. Jeffrey was not with us as he was doing his stint in juvenile hall for his trumped-up truancy violations.

Once again, a *For Sale* sign came up unexpectedly in the front yard of the house I was living in and caring for. The executor of the estate decided to settle the estate. He put the house up for sale. My life was about to change, again.

Kim and I—together now for nine months—and my mother packed up and moved to Kim's home in Hooterville, Utah. The majority of Melinda's and my belongings ended up in the three-car garage, as Kim's house was already full of her furniture.

One morning, Kim, who traveled for work, needed a ride to the airport. Luckily, I went straight back to the house from the airport. When I walked into the house, Melinda was lying next to her walker in a puddle of urine with a phone in her hand. In disbelief, I looked at her and shook my head.

"Mom, why didn't you dial 911, or me? For god's sake, you have the phone in your hand."

"I was talking to Bud when I fell. I did not want to hang up. I knew you would be back soon, so I just waited for you."

Of course, this made no sense to me. I took the phone out of her hand and dialed 911. The paramedics arrived quickly and got her off the floor onto a gurney and took her to the hospital. After X-rays and tests, the doctor figured out she had broken her leg.

## Mother Moved Out

My mother needed immediate surgery that included dozens of pins, screws, and plates. She would then have an extended hospital stay. Later, they would transfer her to a rehabilitation center to teach her how to walk again. She would be there for months.

## Jeffrey Returns

Jeffrey turned eighteen, and they released him from juvenile hall. The harassment stopped, not because he turned eighteen, but because we left Bighorn. He came to live with Kim and me in Hooterville. He got a job at a big box store. He quickly realized he would not be able to support himself.

Jeffrey did research and signed up for heating and air conditioning (HVAC) school. Kim and I helped him with his classes. He read his assignments and then talked about them with us. We all learned about air conditioners, compressors, motors, and pumps. Jeffrey graduated on January 4, 2001. We were enormously proud of him.

I kept my promise to Jeffrey and got him through high school. Now, he had a practical career. Because of my life choices, Jeffrey attended five public school systems, including Hawaii, Utah, Arizona, Washington, and Florida. Not one of these systems addressed his learning disabilities. Thankfully, private schools helped him succeed.

Unfortunately, my insurance paid zero dollars of the expenses. This included special, private, at-risk, and boarding school—also the tattoo cover-up and the car buy-back. I did not pay for the HVAC School; Jeffrey did. Overall, I ended up over $100,000 in debt and filed for bankruptcy. I would do it all again to help Jeffrey achieve his goals.

People, especially my family, never understood, nor did they accept the struggles Jeffrey went through. They never took the time to learn about Jeffrey's disabilities. It broke my heart. I can only imagine how it made Jeffrey feel. It was extremely painful to me when my family belittled Jeffrey and me.

"Why do you baby him?" They said. "There's nothing wrong with him."

Jeffrey's gifts were something that few people have. From an incredibly early age, he was there with a hug if you were sad or cried. He listened to your problems and found a way to comfort you. He convinced you that everything would be okay.

Jeffrey was the most loving person I have ever known. He and Bud always said, *I love you* to me and to each other. They always shared a kiss with me. Sometimes, their friends teased them.

They said, "Shut up; you're just jealous."

Every young man should learn these behaviors; there would be far fewer bullies in our society.

**Another Move**

Kim, offered a job in California in December of 2000, hastened a move and a new adventure. Kim and I packed up and moved to California. Melinda was in rehab in Fallen Meadow, recovering from a broken leg, and Jeffrey was about to graduate from HVAC School. Jeffrey decided he wanted to stay in Utah for a while and work at his new profession.

"Mom, in Fallen Meadow, there will always be air conditioners and heaters that need to be repaired."

When Jeffrey made that decision, I honestly believed it would be an opportunity for him to experience adulthood. Leaving Jeffrey in Utah was a decision I would regret for the rest of my life.

Next thing we knew, the *Soul Train* roared full steam ahead down the track into Arizona on January 3, 2001. The year started out with a *bang*! Just after Kim and I moved to California, *Death #2* slammed into the station, *All Aboard!* The red lights flashed, and the gates crashed down as the *Soul Train* roared into town. Kim's mother, Elaina, died suddenly after suffering a massive stroke.

Unfortunately, Kim was on a flight to Arizona from California when Elaina died. Kim wanted to see her mother one last time before she died. Not getting there in time to see her mother broke Kim's heart.

We wished the *Soul Train* would derail and leave us alone—no more deaths for us. Kim and I were *living the dream* in California. Bud was home, Jeffrey was thinking about moving home, and life was good. 2001 was going to be the year I dreamed of—love and family were finally mine.

PART III

# JEFFREY'S NEVER COMING HOME

## CHAPTER 26

# THE TWILIGHT ZONE

The Next Day Came: March 30, 2001. Day #3 of the *murder* word in our life. Surely the day would be better than the last two days we had barely survived, wouldn't it? It could not get any worse, could it? Why did I continue to ask these stupid questions? Jeffrey repeatedly warned me about this habit of mine. He scolded me that I cursed myself.

As previously directed, I called Detective J. He gave me an address and told me to meet him there at twelve o'clock. Bud entered the address into our TomTom (pre-GPS) as we had no idea where the location was other than in Fallen Meadow.

Kim, Bud, Marisol, and I climbed into our SUV and headed into Fallen Meadow. I have no recollection of who drove. Our hope for the day was to get more answers about the now-confirmed murder of Jeffrey.

Somehow, we erroneously thought we were going to meet Detective J at a police station. To our surprise, we ended up in a residential neighborhood. The address took us to a single-family dwelling with a single car garage facing the street.

"Why would the Detective tell us to meet him here? Are you sure we have the correct address?" I asked.

Bud replied, "Yes, this is exactly where he said to come."

Dumbfounded, we got out of the car and stood on the side of the street. We stared at the houses around us. I am sure we looked out of place. It was clear we did not belong there.

Once again, Artie and his wife Gail showed up. I do not know where, when, or why they were there, but they were. I guess Bud must have told them where we were going and when to be there.

Something did not feel right at all. I felt like somebody punched me in the stomach. I knew in my heart this was a horrible place to be; there was something evil about this place. I usually go with my gut feelings, and this time, my gut told me this was not good.

A very odd thought popped into my head.

"Do you think this is where Jeffrey was murdered?" I asked.

Everyone looked at me, shocked, and then looked around even more confused. We continued to stare at the houses. I do not know how long we stood there.

I asked, "Should I call the detective to see if we are at the wrong address?"

Where was Detective J? Should he not have been here before us? He set the place and the time for this appointment.

**Jeffrey Story**

Suddenly, a funny memory entered my mind about Jeffrey. When Jeffrey had an appointment, he expected the other people to be there at that time. An example would be when Jeffrey had a doctor's appointment.

Jeffrey said, "If I can be on time, then they can be on time."

If his doctor's appointment was at 3:00 p.m., he expected the doctor to see him at 3:00 p.m. If they did not call him before or at 3:00 p.m., he went up to the counter.

Always polite, Jeffrey would say, "Excuse me, my appointment is at 3:00 p.m. It is 3:00 p.m. I would like to be seen now."

The lady behind the counter always looked shocked at him. She replied, "The doctor is behind. You'll have to wait."

Jeffrey said, "If I can be on time, then the doctor can be on time. I will have to reschedule."

People were surprised by his patience and admired his determination that his time was just as valuable as the doctor's.

I am not sure why this memory popped into my head, but I now knew that Jeffrey was there with me, as a new Guardian Angel. Whatever this situation was about to be, Jeffrey would protect me.

**What the Hell?**

Suddenly, the garage door opened at the exact address given to us by Detective J. At first, I thought I was seeing things. It was unclear, but I thought Jeffrey's car was in the garage. I wondered: *How could this be possible?*

The car looked like Jeffrey's car but, in a primer, gray color. Why would somebody cover Jeffrey's car in primer? There were also weird tires on the vehicle.

A man came out of the garage and started to cross the street towards our group. Something felt wrong, and that strange, horrible feeling in my stomach worsened. I could not breathe, and my feet would not move.

The big-shouldered, scruffy, tattooed, and mean-looking guy came over to where we stood. Stupid, we should have gotten back in the cars and locked the doors, but nobody moved.

The guy said, "My name is Jackson. Why are you all staring at my house?"

We continued to stare at the man dumbfounded. Nobody responded.

The man named Jackson said, "I am a friend of Jeff's. He was staying here."

Somehow, I came out of my confusion and found my voice. "Jeff was staying here?" I asked.

He replied, "Yes, are you Jeff's family?"

I said, "Yes, I am his mother. When was Jeffrey staying here?"

He did not answer. He had an agenda and wanted to tell us his side of the story. He continued, "When we got up that morning, Jeff and I decided to get donuts for everybody. Jeff drove his car to the donut shop. When we returned to the house, we pulled into the garage, and Jack Ashe was standing there."

It was unbelievable. We stared at this unknown man who tried to explain an unfathomable story to us. *Where are the detectives who were supposed to meet us?* The whole situation was bazaar. For all we knew, this man murdered Jeffrey.

He persisted, "I started going into the house with the donuts when I heard the murderer (as he described him) Jack Ashe, say '*Hey Jeff.*' Suddenly there was this loud explosion. It took me a second to realize it was a gunshot. My ears were ringing so loudly."

He was trying to make it clear to us that Jack Ashe was the murderer and the one who shot Jeffrey. He wanted us to believe he was not the one who murdered Jeffrey. I felt a very strange vibe from him, so I repeated what he said.

I said, "So this Jack Ashe guy just said, '*Hey Jeff,*' and then he shot him?"

"Yes, when I turned around, I saw the murderer, Jack Ashe, holding the gun. It looked like a shotgun. Then I saw Jeff on the garage floor."

I honestly cannot believe I was able to stand at that point. The man had just casually described the murder of my son.

Once again, my head pounded. Sweat poured down my body, and I shook from head to toe. I thought I was having a panic attack. There had to be more to the story. He would not stop talking.

Jackson continued, "Jeffrey said to Jack Ashe, '*What did you do?*' I ran into the house and hid. I thought he would shoot me next."

What kept me from throwing up or strangling this man was beyond my scope of understanding. I could not believe that he had left Jeffrey shot and dying in the garage, alone with a man who had a gun. It was obvious that Jackson wanted us to believe he was afraid of this man with the gun.

He maintained, "I waited a bit inside the house. When I did not hear anything else, I went back into the garage and checked to see what was happening. The murderer, Jack Ashe, was gone. I could not find a phone, so I ran next door and told the neighbor to dial 911. The ambulance took Jeff to the hospital."

Jackson seemed to have this story memorized. He kept using the name Jack Ashe. He even tried to look remorseful and sad. He said, "I am deeply sorry for your loss. You can come over to the house and wait for the police to arrive."

*How does this man know the police were even coming?* He did not even ask us why we were there. *What am I supposed to say to this man? Is it all a lie to cover his own ass?* For all we knew, he was the murderer.

Jackson made it noticeably clear to us that he blamed it on this other guy named Jack Ashe. There were so many unanswered questions. We had no idea who this man really was. *Why are we here?*

## The House of Murder

Things got even crazier. Bud or his father made the decision to walk over to the house; the rest of us followed. The reality hit me like a sledgehammer that this was the *House of Murder*, as I would forever refer to it.

*My baby, Jeffrey, died right here, in the driveway we were walking on.* We followed the man called Jackson into the garage. This place was the very spot where *somebody* murdered Jeffrey.

Once we entered the garage, it became clear to Bud and me that it was indeed Jeffrey's car. Why it looked the way it did, we had no idea. We both stared at the car in disbelief.

Bud mumbled, "What the hell happened to Jeffrey's car?"

Next thing we knew, there was a woman in the garage. She said, "My name is Ariana. I am a friend of Jeff's. He lived with me for approximately three months."

*What the hell is this girl talking about?* When could this have been? Kim and I had been in California for two months, so when did Jeffrey live with all these people? She seemed to want to talk to me.

She asked, "Why is Jeff's car painted in primer?"

I answered her, "That is a great question. I was wondering the same thing myself."

She snapped, "I don't know why. There doesn't appear to be any damage to the car."

I had a tough time trying to put all this together in my mind. Everything swirled. Nothing made sense. *Who are these people?* This whole thing smelled.

I mumbled to myself, "Why are we here? Where are the detectives?"

I said aloud, "There are a lot of things that just do not add up or make sense to me. The guy said this Jack Ashe person shot Jeffrey. Why would he have shot Jeffrey? If you knew Jeffrey at all, then you know that he would have given anybody anything that he had."

Ariana looked at me, dumbly. She said, "I have no idea. He is a crazy tattoo artist. He does a lot of crystal meth."

*Why am I having a conversation with this woman I do not even know?* She was talking about my son, who was now dead. *Does she not know he is lying in a funeral home?* I did not want to be here any longer. *Oh my god*! The woman was talking again.

She rattled on, "I cannot believe the police left me here with all this blood to clean up. There was blood everywhere. Don't you think they should have sent somebody over here to clean up all this blood? Do I look like I am a fucking maid or cleaning lady to you?"

*Shut the hell up!* I wanted to scream.

That was the final straw. I needed to get out of that garage. I wanted to get away from these people. I wanted to know who they really were and how they were really involved in Jeffrey's murder.

Death and evil hung in the air in this house, this garage, on these people. I walked out into the yard; at least the air was moving. *Can I get some more air into my lungs?* There seemed to be no air to breathe.

Everything around me appeared distorted. I could not believe the things I had just heard or seen.

Questions swirled in my head. *What were the police thinking when they sent me to this House of Murder? What force of the Universe brings a mother to the spot where her son laid alone and died? Why are the police forcing me to meet these people? How can I even listen to this woman bitch about cleaning up the blood of my son?*

I would have given my very life to have my son back. I wanted his blood back in him, not to hear a bitch complaining about having to clean up my dead son's blood. *His blood should not be on the floor of a garage or in a driveway. It should be in his healthy, alive body.*

Was there any humanity left in the world? I did not know. How could I have stood in the exact spot where somebody murdered my son? I will never get the scene of this nightmare out of my head.

*If only my head would fragment into smithereens, like Humpty Dumpty, they would never put it back together again.* How had I ever ended up at the House of Murder?

All I knew for sure was that I did not want to be at this house. Hell, for that matter, I did not even want to be on this Earth. Had the world gone mad? Did *They* expect me to endure this nightmare? I could barely breathe or stand.

Where the hell were the detectives who told us to meet them? Did they really have the victim's mother come to the very house where the murder of her child took place? What the hell was wrong with the Universe?

CHAPTER 27

# POLICE INCOMPETENCY

Finally, a police vehicle arrived at this nightmare scene. I had no idea what to say to these men, or what to say about them. As an ex-law enforcement officer, I had to question whether these two men had overstayed their time in their profession, as they seemed inept in possessing any empathy or compassion for the family who lost a child.

There truly was no excuse for their behavior or their treatment of a victim's mother and family. No one should ever receive the mistreatment we endured. Jeffrey was the victim of a senseless murder. Jeffrey was a human being. I was a mother who just lost her child. Bud lost his brother and best friend. Jeffrey never harmed anybody in his entire life; we deserved respect and dignity.

The treatment we received from the Fallen Meadow police was unnecessary torture. If I had not been heartbroken and consumed by grief, I would have told them exactly how cruel they were to my family and me. There was absolutely no excuse for what they did during this whole nightmare of Jeffrey's murder.

Detective J and Detective T got out of their car and walked over to our group. Detective J said, "Thank you for meeting us here. I asked you here so you could take possession of Jeffrey's vehicle. They need it out of the garage. Here are the keys."

We stared at these men in utter disbelief and horror. This outrageousness was just another slap in the face, a knife stabbed in my back.

*Picking up a car is the only freaking reason we are at this House of Murder!*

Could they not have moved the vehicle to any different location? Hell, they could have driven it around the block. Why did the victim's family have to come to the very place somebody murdered their child to pick up a *thing*?

Were these men so lazy and inhumane they could not have managed this situation differently? Did they even think about what they were doing to my family and me? No! Detective J dropped the keys to Jeffrey's car into my hand.

*The Devil himself placed a ball of fire into the palm of my hand.*

I stared at them; the keys burned my hand. There were no words to describe the finality these keys brought to me. I handed the keys over to Bud. Unsure of what to do with them either, he stared at me and then at the keys.

Why had I just transferred the fires of hell into Bud's hand?

Bud asked with tears running down his face, "What should I do Mom?"

How I remained calm and did not scream at these two men, I will never know.

"Bud, get Jeffrey's car the f**k out of that place."

I do not know how Bud did it, but he went back into the garage. He walked around the car and checked the condition of the vehicle. He got in the car and surprisingly, it started. We had no idea about the car's mechanical condition.

Bud backed it out into the street, just to get it out of that garage and away from the House of Murder.

"Why is Jeffrey's car here? Why are we here at the scene of my child's murder?" I demanded.

"We did not have any reason to take his car into evidence, so we left it here." Detective J responded arrogantly.

"Are you kidding me? Why would you make us come to the very place where somebody murdered my son, just to pick up his car? Could you not have taken the car anywhere else?" I asked.

"We had no reason to move it." Detective J replied.

## Questions and More Questions

Honestly, I do not know how I continued to stand or breathe. Somehow, I held my anger. Surprisingly, I did not get myself arrested by telling this ass what he could do and how I felt about him. It was not worth it to let these guys know how deeply they hurt me. I still needed the answers I came to get, or we would have just walked away. Exasperated with him, I kept my fury under control and asked my questions.

"What exactly happened to Jeffrey? Was Jeffrey alive when he was taken to the hospital?"

"Based on the close range and the extent of his injuries, there was no way possible for Jeff to have survived."

That did not really answer my question, but this guy never answered the question I asked.

"Do you know if he suffered? Do you know if he said anything?"

"We were told that Jeffrey said, '*What have you done?*'"

"Where are Jeffrey's other possessions?" I asked.

Detective T said, "The items pertinent to the case are in evidence. Anything else is in his car or in this house. Other than that, I have no idea."

These men pissed me off so much. "Did you find his driver's license? What about his passport? Did the person steal this stuff?" I asked.

"We did not find any of those items. Let me check the report." Detective T responded.

The detective flipped through his metal clipboard with papers.

"Jeffrey had a Gerber 650 knife with a black handle, $4.00 in U.S. currency, fifty-one cents U.S. currency, a handwritten letter, a note, a black wallet with decals, a sealed box of Marlboro 100s cigarettes, a Freedom pager, a Motorola pager, a bottle of Visine, and Bubble Tape 6 Feet chewing gum in a sealed container. No identification—neither a driver's license nor a passport," he replied.

It would not matter what he said, it would never bring Jeffrey back. I was so tired of being brave and acting strong. I wanted to lie down on the ground and die in the exact same spot where Jeffrey died.

I ask one final question, "What do we need to do next?"

"There is nothing else to do. We will continue to search for Jack Ashe."

I needed to get away from these people before I said something very stupid. I said to Kim, "I am done. We must go. I cannot take any more."

Marisol told me later in the car how shocked she was to see that while I talked to the police officers, Artie appeared so calm and uninvolved. That was no surprise to me, as he had never been involved in Jeffrey's life. "Everyone else appeared to be in shock, yet Artie seemed oblivious to what was going on, or how the police treated you and Bud."

"I did not notice. It took everything I had left not to lose my temper with the two police officers, or the other idiots who stood by watching the charade." I said.

There were not enough words in the dictionary to describe the inexplicable scene. There were no interpretations or excuses that made this police behavior forgivable. I had no idea how I would ever continue my life. It certainly would never be the same again.

CHAPTER 28

# WILL THIS NIGHTMARE END?

We walked away from the House of Murder in utter shock. After a brief discussion, we decided Bud would drive Jeffrey's car to my work for the time being. It would be safe and secure there. Thankfully, Bud offered to drive it, as I do not think I would have been capable of handling it.

Artie decided to ride with Bud, which was nice, since Bud would have been alone in his dead brother's car. The car, covered in fingerprint dust as the police had fingerprinted it for evidence, was a mess. It would be a project to clean the inside of the vehicle, but that would be someday down the road. Bud was okay with getting dirty.

Shaken to my core, my world was off balance. I could not find my direction. There was no grounding within this murder thing. After we got Jeffrey's car secured at my work, the six of us decided to get something to eat. I vaguely remembered sitting at the table. I do not think I ate any food.

We shared Jeffrey stories. Artie and Gail knew little about Jeffrey; I thought they should learn what a wonderful, loving young man he was. I never understood why Artie and Gail came all that way for a funeral, for a son Artie never took the time to know. I wondered: If Jeffrey had not called him that summer three years before and asked him to dinner at the truck stop if Artie would have bothered. Oh well, he bears his own guilt and grief.

Bud, now 21 years old, had not seen his father since he was fifteen years old and lived in Wisconsin his freshman year in high school. However, his father kicked him out of his home for reasons unknown to me. Bud had spent weeks living on the streets of Red Water, Wisconsin. He finally called me in Arizona, and I flew him home to live with me until he joined the U.S. Navy.

After we ate, Kim and I said our goodbyes to Gail and Artie for the last time. I wondered: Would Artie spend time with Bud and learn what a wonderful, strong man he became? Could Artie be a father to his only son now? I could not waste any more of my time with these people. I had absolutely nothing to say to them.

This had been the most numbing, nauseating, and horrible three days of my life. I could not get it out of my head that somebody murdered my child and left him to die alone. The thought made me sick to my stomach.

Bud spent ten more minutes with his father. He was no longer the boy his father kicked out. He had served his country in the Navy for over five years and was a full-time college student. Bud was a truly kind soul, like Jeffrey, and was very forgiving. He spoke politely with his father.

**Back at the Condo**

This had been another long and horrific day. We found Lynette, waiting with her children and their families. The poodles were ecstatic to see us. We relayed all the horrific and dreadful details of what we endured during our trip to Fallen Meadow. The story about what happened was unfathomable. All we could do was tell the truth. There was no way to make this crap up.

Lynette was livid. She said, "I cannot believe they had you go to the very place where Jeffrey was murdered. Were the police out of their freaking minds?"

"I have no idea why they would take a parent to the murder scene. This has been the second-worst day of my life." I answered.

"I thought yesterday was unbelievable, but this was stupid, if nothing else. How could they have you go there?" Lynnette asked.

"I was actually standing in the spot where Jeffrey was shot and killed by some lunatic on drugs. It was like a scene from a horror movie. I will never forget it."

"Well, you are a stronger woman than me. I do not think I could have gone there. I know I would not have held my tongue with the way those detectives treated you. That is just freaking ridiculous." Lynette replied.

"Then, they just handed me the keys to Jeffrey's car. They told us we had to move the car as the people wanted it out of their garage." I said.

"That was inhumane!" Lynette replied.

"Thank god, Bud was able to drive Jeffrey's car. Kim thought to leave the car at my work for now. It will be safe there. It's not like I could drive it."

Bud said, "It was like Jeffrey was in the car when we drove it over to Mom's work. It was the strangest thing. My dad tried to talk to me like he knew Jeffrey. It was such bullshit. I knew Mom would want me to not be rude to him. I just did my best to drive and not cry."

I said, "Bud, he has his own hell to live in. Do not worry about him. You never know, he may reach out to you and try to be a father. Who knows? Now that he lost one son, he might want to get to know the other one."

**Bud and Marisol**

Bud said, "Marisol and I have to go home tomorrow. She applied for a permanent position with our district. She has an interview."

"Awesome news, Marisol. I think Kim and I will stay another day or two. I need to see if there is anything we need to do."

Bud and Marisol left the next morning for California. Marisol later told me they drove home in silence to the Captain Island house.

Marisol later told me the story in her words. She said, "Bud and I slept for a couple hours, and he took me to the interview the next morning."

Bud said, "Marisol, I know you can do this. You are qualified for this job. Please do it for me and in memory of Jeffrey."

"I will, Bud, I promise. I will do my absolute best."

"Kathy, you would have been proud of me. I raised my head up, walked powerfully into the building, and aced the job interview."

Marisol got the job. She still works for the community college system in the Poison Oak, California area.

She concluded, "Things were never the same for Bud after Jeffrey's death. Bud always had a sad look in his eyes after Jeffrey died. When he thought you weren't looking, the sadness went even deeper."

The Next Day Came. They continued to come.

CHAPTER 29

# LOST IN LIMBO

I could not wrap my mind around the fact that Jeffrey was dead. Sleep was elusive to me. The images of Jeffrey dead on that gurney burned the inside of my eyelids every time I blinked or closed my eyes to sleep. It was my own personal horror movie.

We watched the news, hoping they would find Jack Ashe. I really was not sure what I was supposed to do *this* day or any day after March 26, 2001. I felt so lost and alone. My baby was gone.

Kim and I stayed in Bighorn for two more days. Kim, Lynette, and I sat down for breakfast and discussed what to do next.

**Obituary**

Lynette asked, "Are you going to put an obituary in the Bighorn Newspaper, or the Fallen Meadow paper?"

Kim asked, "Kathy, what do you think about it?"

Jeffrey deserved an obituary. I believed the local police, and even the town itself, had a part in the death of Jeffrey. Their petty juvenile harassment resulted in the loss of a good soul. I believed in my heart if they would have just left Jeffrey alone when we first came back to Utah, things would have turned out differently.

"Oh, we should definitely let this place know exactly what happened to Jeffrey. They could have done so much to help him. Instead, they ruined his life. Jeffrey ended up in a driveway with three bad guys, one who murdered him. They have his blood on their hands. Maybe it will change the way they do business."

Kim said, "Okay then, that is what we will do."

Lynette said, "That would be a fantastic result, if something good came out of the senseless death of a young man who had so much to live for."

"They will never again harass my son, Jeffrey, because he is dead."

> Jeffrey, 18 years old, died in a homicide Monday, March 26, 2001, in Fallen Meadow, Utah. He was a long-time resident of the Bighorn area. As a member of the Bighorn Swim Team, he won dozens of trophies and medals.
>
> Jeffrey was born in Tabor, Wisconsin. He graduated from Front Range High School and recently completed heating and air conditioning school in Fallen Meadow, Utah. Jeffrey was also a certified diver, certified lifeguard, and certified scuba diver.
>
> Survivors include his mother Kathy and brother Bud, father Artie, Grandmother Melinda, and Grandfather Torrance.
>
> The family held private services Thursday, March 29, 2001. Cremation followed. Jeffrey will find his eternal rest in the waters he loved in Hawaii.

Did the police see the obituary? Who knows? But I hope they did. Did the police care about what happened to Jeffrey? I doubt it. Could the murder of one of their longtime residents at eighteen years old change the practices of the local police department? That was the only hope I could find for the children of Bighorn, Utah.

Jeffrey's life deserved recognition and honor. He may have been on this Earth for a truly abbreviated time, but he affected the lives of dozens of people, including myself. Jeffrey was a kind, loving soul. His kindness and love are the reason I am still here today.

There were dozens of times the responsibilities of raising my two sons weighed me down, but Jeffrey's love and care kept me alive. I can and will tell Jeffrey stories for the rest of my life. Believe me, he gave me hundreds of stories to tell.

Kim and I stayed with Lynette for a couple more days. I was not functioning well. I could not sleep, and I did not want to eat. The mental stress was unbearable, and the physical stress began to take its toll.

Jagger and Angel supplied unconditional love. It gave me a little peace to sit and hold them. I thought of how Jeffrey loved his poodles. I did my best to find pieces of sane ground on which to stand. I needed something to hang onto.

The police told me they arrested Jack Ashe on April 2, 2001. Detective J. informed me that the prosecuting attorney would contact me in three weeks. He reiterated there was nothing else we could do. That was the last I ever heard from Detective J.

**Headed Home**

At that point, I was numb, tired, exhausted, and heartbroken. I wanted to go home. I had a new home with Kim, Bud, and the poodles. There was nothing more I could do for Jeffrey but wait. We had to wait to hear from the district attorney.

I wondered what their plans were for Jack Ashe. The police were certain he was the one who murdered Jeffrey. I was not sure how they came to that conclusion, or if they would be able to prove it. There was still something fishy to me about the whole story those men told us at the House of Murder.

At least we knew where Jeffrey was. Lynette would pick up Jeffrey's ashes at the funeral home when they completed his cremation. They told us the process took a week to ten days.

*How can this be? All that remains of my child is a box of ashes.*

We loaded Jagger and Angel, along with their crates and the suitcases into the back of the truck.

Lynette said, "Well, Kathy, I hate to see you go, but if there is anything I can do to help, please just let me know."

"Thank you for all your help, especially for picking me up that horrible night."

"I don't know how you are ever going to survive this. Stay strong. You are a much stronger woman than I could ever be."

As we got ready to leave, Kim asked me, "Are you sure you want to drive? I can drive, and you can rest." She hates to drive, so it was nice of her to offer.

"No, I will drive. It will give me something to do besides think."

"Do you want to listen to an audiobook or just talk?"

"Let's just talk for now. It's better to keep my mind busy."

I realized I would not be able to handle traveling the regular route home to California. We normally took the route that brought us directly up the mountain pass. It was just too raw. Memories flashed of that horrible night. My life changed forever at the top of the mountain pass. I said, "Let's go the other route into California. I think it would be best to avoid the mountain pass for right now."

JEFFREY | 155

"That's a great idea. Besides, we have not been that way in a long time. It will be a change of scenery for us. We can see what's new and all the changes."

The trip went by very quickly. We stopped for lunch. We talked about all the family members we saw while in Bighorn. Even though we saw these people for a horrible, unbelievable reason, it was still nice. It would have been better to have all my family for support, but I never had a normal family, so that was nothing new.

Kim and I decided to discuss our trip to Hawaii. We would take Jeffrey to his final resting place in Maui, Hawaii. Kim was the trip planner and organizer. She would check her work schedule to see when she could go. She would find out from Bud and Marisol when they were available.

Together, the four of us would take the *Huge Expensive Vacation,* for Jeffrey. That trip was supposed to be for me when I died, not my children. How had the world gotten it all wrong?

**Stage Shows**

When Kim and I arrived home after the nightmare week of hell, Kim suddenly remembered that we bought tickets months before to see *Mamma Mia* at the theatre in Poison Oak on April 7. She had waited for months to see this musical. I hate musicals or plays, but I go along for Kim's sake.

Besides, if we paid hundreds of dollars to see the musical, we were going to see it. Kim felt this would give us something to do and would be something to occupy my mind besides the tragedy spinning in it.

I would highly recommend, if someone murdered your child, not to attend a musical about someone else's child's wedding and childbirth. I cried the entire time. The whole play sent me into a deeper depression. It reminded me how there would never be a wedding for Jeffrey. There would never be the joy of his children, my grandchildren.

Kim loved the play, although she knew it was sad for me. She loved the theatrical experience and enjoyed spending the time with me.

Somehow, I had to figure out what the rest of my life would be like without Jeffrey in it. Bud and I had to figure out a way to make it through this disaster together. The *Three Musketeers* now became *Two of a Kind*. Our lives had changed forever.

The Next Day Came. They would not stop coming.

# CHAPTER 30
# OFFICIAL REPORT

April 10, 2001. I received an official copy of the police investigation, as follows:

An officer arrived at 0630 hours military time and found the victim, Jeffrey, lying on the ground near the garage door and driveway. The officer described his wounds and condition in detail.

The officer stayed with Jeffrey until the arrival of the paramedics. He was conscious; however, he did not make any statements. They transported Jeffrey by ambulance to the hospital.

The doctor pronounced Jeffrey dead at 0705 hours on March 26, 2001. They performed an autopsy on Jeffrey, and it was determined that he died from a shotgun wound to the abdomen. The weapon used to kill Jeffrey was a Western Field pump-action shotgun, 12-gauge, with a wooden pistol-grip buttstock or sawed-off shotgun. The autopsy concluded that Jeffrey's death was a homicide.

The man named Jackson told the exact same story to the police that he told us when we stood in front of his house. However, later in the report, it said that a man named Ryker, Jackson's relative, came forward with his statement. This statement contradicted what the man named Jackson said.

This was Ryker's story. Ryker said, "I witnessed the shooting. Jeff and Jack Ashe went to get the donuts. Jeff handed the donuts to me. When Jeff turned around, Jack Ashe shot him with the shotgun."

He states that Jeff said, "Oh no, you f**ked up. What did you do?"

Ryker ran into the house and hid. He sent Jackson out to the garage to see what happened.

Jackson told Ryker, "Call 911 and report the shooting."

Ryker called the police, but he did not wait for the police as he had warrants for his arrest. So, the report confirmed the two men lied about what happened at the House of Murder. They both implicated Jack Ashe, the third man.

The only clear fact was that my son Jeffrey was dead, and the other men involved appeared to have different stories as to what exactly happened and who murdered Jeffrey.

The report concluded that the police arrested Jack Ashe on April 2, 2001 and charged him with murder with a deadly weapon, and robbery with a deadly weapon. According to the report, Jack Ashe had one thing to say.

"I'll wait for my attorney," he said.

CHAPTER 31

# FLASHBACK

People often asked me how I knew cremation was what Jeffrey wanted when he died. They thought it strange I would have a discussion with my fifteen-year-old son about what I wanted when I died. They thought it even stranger that he would decide about cremation for himself.

The story came about when Jeffrey, my mother, and I were on vacation in Hawaii, in 1997, for Jeffrey's spring break. The three of us got up early and made the drive to a black sand beach on Maui. It was one of our favorite places to go every time we visited the islands.

*Jeffrey Above His Black Sand Beach*

The area was beyond beautiful with clear turquoise blue water. As we floated around in the warm water and relaxed, we talked about life, and the subject of death came up.

"Jeffrey, when I die, I want you and Bud to have me cremated. Then, you and Bud take this Huge Expensive Vacation and bring my ashes to this very spot," I said.

"Okay! Mom, I do not want you to ever die. I would miss you too much, but that would be cool. We can bring you here," Jeffrey replied.

"I want you both to celebrate my life, not cry and be sad. The trip would be an all-expense paid vacation since I have a large amount of life insurance. You two could ride Harley Davidson Motorcycles, scuba dive (if you get certified), go to a luau, and surf. Make sure to eat a lot of good seafood," I said.

"That sounds like an exciting time. It would only be better if you were there with us, Mom," Jeffrey replied.

"Jeffrey, you and Bud should tell lots of funny and crazy stories about me."

Jeffrey laughed and said, "Well, that is easy to do. There are lots of crazy and funny stories about you."

With that, I dunked him underwater. He came up, dunked me, and we laughed. "Okay, cool Mom, we'll do it. When I die, I want to come here too, so we can be together."

"That would be cool Jeffrey, but not anytime soon. Somebody else will have to make a trip to Hawaii to bring you here since I will already be here."

"I'm sure that will be no problem, Mom. Who wouldn't want a vacation to Hawaii?" Jeffrey answered.

About this time, Melinda decided to join the conversation.

"Well then, if that is what you two are going to do, then I want to come here too. I want to be with both of you," Melinda said.

Jeffrey laughed again and splashed water at her. "Grandma, you can't come here, you already have your apartment in Bighorn."

"Well, somebody else can go in my apartment then. I do not want to be in Bighorn all by myself. I want to be here in Hawaii. You know I have always loved it here," Melinda replied.

Everyone knew the story of my mom's apartment. Back in the early 1980s, she bought a mausoleum crypt in the Bighorn Cemetery. She always referred to it as her *apartment*. The crypt still sits empty.

Jeffrey finished the death conversation. "Ladies, we do not have to worry about any of us coming back here as ashes for now. We need to enjoy our vacation," Jeffrey said.

"Exactly, we can do some snorkeling and see some fish. Then, we are going to Mama's Fish House for excellent seafood! I'm getting hungry," I agreed.

Jeffrey and I loved tropical islands and warm ocean water. We traveled to Hawaii, Tahiti, the Grand Caymans, and the Florida Keys together for scuba diving trips. He had a never-ending love of the water. I had an unending love for him.

That was how I knew Jeffrey wanted cremation and where he wanted his final resting place to be.

*Jeffrey Surfing in Maui*

CHAPTER 32

# BACK TO WORK

Life made plans for us that we did not plan on at all! I never imagined that I would outlive one of my children. I had no idea how I was supposed to continue with this hole in my heart and soul. It was nice to be home with Kim and Bud; however, we had our hands full helping Bud through the loss of Jeffrey.

Kim coordinated the trip to Maui, Hawaii, with Bud and Marisol for the Huge Expensive Vacation.

Kim said, "I invited Bud and Marisol for dinner this weekend when you get back from work. We can discuss our dates and plans for the trip."

"Thanks, Kim. We can eat at the house and just spend time with them."

Kim said, "Perfect, are you ready to head to the airport?"

*Author note:* The murder of Jeffrey was prior to September 11, 2001. Flying in the United States of America was a simple procedure.

Kim dropped me off fifteen to twenty minutes before the flight took off at Poison Oak International Airport for work on Monday mornings and picked me up on Thursday evenings.

Kim printed my boarding pass at home. I walked in the door and right up to the gate. Then, I showed my boarding pass to the attendant at the gate and walked onto a plane for Fallen Meadow.

## Back to Work

With my irrational sense of responsibility, combined with the fact that the company did not have a replacement driver who could take over my route, I felt obligated to fulfill my work commitment.

So, on April 9, twelve days after the murder of my son, Jeffrey, I took a Southwest flight to Fallen Meadow, Utah, and officially went back to work.

What the hell was I thinking?

In my mind, I knew I did not have the mental capacity to drive 80,000 pounds down the highways of America again. The word *zombie* described my state of mind, but nobody besides me knew the truth. I was not sure how I was even upright and breathing.

My ability to function during the most stressful or chaotic times always amazed me. This capability had fooled people, schools, doctors, and the police about the amount of alcohol I consumed during my life. I always was a very functional, polite, and responsible alcoholic. I used these same tactics to convince people I was okay when I was not functioning well at all.

Murder, however, was a whole new concept for me to figure out in my subconscious mind. My brain knew how to react and behave with the consumption of copious amounts of alcohol and still appear normal in society.

My brain had no strategy for responding and appearing normal when it came to the murder of my son. Appearing strong and together exhausted me. It was a struggle to keep upright.

My thoughts were of revenge, anger, hatred, and contempt for the unjust justice system. The thoughts in my head were not good, but they were mine. I tried to rationalize that they were normal for the situation I went through. *Right?*

## What Not to Say

The following list described eight of the things people said to me about my life when I appeared in public after the murder of my son that did not help me at all. I had more, but you can get the idea.

1. You need to go back to work.
2. Aren't you done crying yet?
3. You need to keep busy.
4. He is in a better place.
5. You need to keep your mind occupied.
6. Life goes on.
7. You need to get over this.
8. He got to go home and is with God.

Can I just say people who have never lost a child have no idea what the hell they are talking about?

They tried to help, right? I know in their hearts they believed they comforted me. It might have even been good advice years later but not right after my child was violently and senselessly murdered.

Truthfully, I should not have gone back to work in the mental or the physical shape I was in. After landing at Fallen Meadow International Airport, I took a cab over to the distribution center. I had left my motorcycle there the night Lynette picked me up.

A huge shock hit me when I saw Jeffrey's car sitting in the parking lot. I had forgotten it was at my work. It amazed me how my mind worked to protect me from the pain. It took my breath away.

Seeing the car in the lot started my mind racing: *How am I ever going to deal with the loss of Jeffrey?* It was so unfair. Jack Ashe had committed five crimes with a gun and was still on this Earth? Why should Jack Ashe have a good old time in this world after robbing and murdering my son?

I could not go over to the car or even look at it, so I went straight into the distribution center. Everyone was glad to see me. They shared their condolences and talked about the story on the television news and in the newspapers. It continued to be in the news for weeks. They were up to date on the arrest of Jack Ashe. I really was not in the mood to talk about it, but I did my best to answer their questions.

Finally, I said, "I'd better go check out my truck and head to California."

Pre-loaded before my arrival, my truck and trailer were ready to go. I completed the required-by-law pre-trip inspection. I drove down to the truck stop and weighed the axles on my tractor-trailer. It was out of balance, so I needed to slide the axles on the trailer to adjust the weight.

This was a process that changed the wheel location on the trailer to distribute the weight in the trailer to another axle. Each axle had a certain weight limit by law. If it is not correct and the truck stops at a scale, the driver receives a ticket. Until the weight issue resolved, the truck stayed at the scale.

Since I had performed this procedure for years, I was able to get through this process on remote control. Once the weight on each axle was correct, I filled fuel in the tractor and the tank for the refrigerated unit (reefer unit) on the trailer.

Before I left the truck stop, I picked up snacks for my trip. All the snacks left in my truck before Jeffrey's murder went in the trash. They had been sitting in my truck for a couple of weeks in over one-hundred-degree temperatures.

**Flashback and Panic Attack**

Things were going well. I filled out my logbook and started out on the interstate. In no time at all, I was at the bottom of the mountain pass in California. Unexpectedly, my mind replayed the trip when I learned of Jeffrey's murder.

My heart raced and I hyperventilated. I felt like I could not breathe. *Oh my god*! I was in a full-blown anxiety attack and once again driving a truck.

I said aloud, "Stay strong; you can do this. Do not forget you have people depending on you. Buck the hell up."

I was not sure who these people were who depended on me, but there must have been somebody. I took a deep breath, shifted gears, and focused on the road and traffic. Somehow, I kept driving. I managed to stay in my lane and did not do damage to any other drivers. I took deep breaths and continued to talk to myself.

I repeated aloud, "Keep focused; you can do this. It is going to be okay."

Guess what happened when I got to the top of the mountain and saw the exit for Kelso Road? Yep, you guessed it.

*Jeffrey died again!*

I needed to stop, but I could not, nor would I ever, take the exit for Kelso Road again. I took the next exit, parked, and cried. *How am I ever going to get my life back together again?*

Life was so unfair. I worked so hard to get Jeffrey grown up and through school. I wondered: What had I ever done to deserve this? Would I ever find a level of sanity in my life? Once again, there was only me to drive this stupid truck. I dug deep. I mean extraordinarily deep. Somehow, I found my functioning, dysfunctional self.

I said aloud, "Kathy, you are an adult. You have another child that needs you. Put yourself back together. People expect you to be strong."

With my eyes closed, I took a dozen deep breaths. Before I started to drive again, I remembered Lynette's advice. I got out of my truck, yelled, and kicked the tires to get my anger under control. Back in the truck, the next stop was Waterman Junction for a restroom break and coffee. Then, it was on to Rancho Santiago and much-needed sleep.

The rest of the week went a little better. The mental stress was unbelievable. My head went around and around, replaying everything that had happened in the two weeks prior. My mind would not stop spinning.

**Headed Home**

I made it through the week. I returned to the distribution center and parked my truck. I said my goodbyes, got on the motorcycle, and surprisingly, the motorcycle started. I headed to the airport as I could not wait to get home. I needed to see Kim, Bud, and the poodles.

Kim picked me up in Poison Oak at the airport. We stopped at one of our favorite restaurants for dinner. We talked about my trips for the week. I described what happened when I got to the mountain pass and how the flashback of the night of Jeffrey's murder felt so real.

Kim suggested, "Maybe you should ask if your company would let you trade routes with another driver for a while. Can you go back to your Texas route? I am sure they would understand under the circumstances."

I agreed, "That's a great idea. I need time for things to settle down. I will call the company headquarters tomorrow and explain my situation."

When I called the corporate offices, they were more than understanding and happy to let me take a different route. For the next month, I took the run to Waterloo, Texas. I flew into Fallen Meadow, got my truck, and headed south through Utah to Arizona. No more nightmares of the mountain pass.

# Change of Scenery

Without fail, on every trip to Waterloo, Texas, I had one or more blown tires on the trailer I pulled. Often, I had no idea there was a flat tire on the trailer. Various times, people pulled up next to me, honked their horn, and waved to let me know that something happened on the back of my trailer.

Sure enough, I would have another flat tire. Occasionally, when a tire blew, I heard the explosion of the tire inside the tractor. At night, I saw sparks flying out from the back of the trailer as the steel belts of the tire sparked on the road.

A blown tire on a semi-truck is not like a flat tire on a car. The driver needs a professional to change the tire. Even worse, these tires always seemed to blow in the middle of *nowhere* west Texas. It took hours for the repair truck to arrive and repair the tire. I experienced at least a dozen flat tires in Texas.

I spent hours on the side of the road with nowhere to go. Too much time was not good for me. Time alone was not the friend of a grieving mother. Suddenly, I remembered the saying, *Time heals all wounds.* Well let me tell you, that was bullshit, plain and simple. Time was not doing anything for me but driving me crazy. Whoever said that obviously did not experience a child murdered.

I played a game of would have, could have, and should have for hours in my head. I thought about Jeffrey. Did he suffer? Did he have anything he wanted to say to me? Was he angry with me for not bringing him to California with me? Would he still be alive if I forced him to come to California? Would Jeffrey ever forgive me?

My functioning, dysfunctional brain kept me moving down the highways of America.

The Next Day Came. It continued to come.

CHAPTER 33

# JEFFREY'S HOME

Lynette picked Jeffrey's ashes up at the funeral home in Fallen Meadow and took him to her condominium in Bighorn as we had arranged at the funeral home on that horrible day. Shocked and surprised by the experience of picking up a loved one's ashes at a funeral home, she called us right away. She wanted to let us know that Jeffrey was with her.

Lynette said, "I had no idea how heavy Jeffrey would be."

Shocked at her statement, having never had a child cremated, I had no idea how to react. I said, "Wow, I never thought about that either."

She went on, "Before the funeral director handed me the cloth bag, he told me that in the bag, there was a cardboard box with a plastic container inside that held Jeffrey's ashes. When he handed it to me, I almost dropped it."

I was not sure how to react to that comment either, but it made sense why the funeral director said that to her. I said, "Well, Jeffrey was a big guy. He was six-foot-three and around 200 pounds. I guess that would mean a lot of ashes, right?"

That was really the reply to the first statement of Jeffrey being heavy, but I think it finally sunk into my brain. We did our best to navigate unchartered waters.

"I am coming over to California to see Lexie and her family. I will stop by your house on Friday and drop Jeffrey off," Lynette said.

I thought about this for a second. We had not really talked about what we were going to do with Jeffrey until we took him to Hawaii. I never thought about him just being in the house as ashes. It would be good to have him home with us for a while.

"That would be a great idea," I said. "Thank you very much, Lynette. I appreciate you doing this for me. I honestly do not know how I make it through each day."

Lynette said, "Kathy, you are doing fine considering all you've been through. Just keep plugging along."

"Lynette, I have no choice. Bud and Marisol are coming over tonight so we can plan the Huge Expensive Vacation to take Jeffrey to Maui. I want to get Jeffrey settled in his final resting place."

The Next Day Comes. They just keep coming; it never stops.

CHAPTER 34

# HUGE EXPENSIVE VACATION

Kim, Bud, Marisol, and I planned our trip to Hawaii. We planned the Huge Expensive Vacation on April 26. Jeffrey died on March 26. We would lay him to rest on that beautiful black sand beach on May 26. Anyone seeing a pattern here?

We placed Jeffrey's ashes on the dresser in the master bedroom. I wanted to have him near me until we took him to Maui.

I wanted Jeffrey alive. I would have given my life for him to be alive again.

May 26$^{th}$ came quickly. With suitcases packed, we headed to the airport. We were not sure what to do with Jeffrey. This was something we had not thought about in planning. We finally decided to put Jeffrey's ashes in a backpack. We knew we would keep Jeffrey with us and carry him onto the plane.

There was no way I would risk losing him as checked baggage. The only stipulation we learned from the airlines was that Jeffrey needed to be in a sealed container, which would go through the X-ray machine. He was in a plastic container, so that was fine. We also carried a copy of his death certificate. We put that in the backpack with his ashes.

Truthfully, we did not know how to manage this whole situation. I reacted with dry sarcastic humor in uncomfortable situations. Sometimes my dry, sarcastic humor shocked people, but this was what got me through the catastrophes in my life. I inherited this dry, sarcastic humor from Melinda.

> *Do not judge my path; you haven't walked in my shoes . . .*
> *or ridden my broom. ~A.M. Galdorecraeft*

We loaded Jeffrey into the car and seat belted him in. When we arrived at Poison Oak International Airport, Bud decided he would be the one to take care of Jeffrey. He threw the backpack up over his shoulder, and off we went.

I could tell Bud was scared and nervous, but he needed to keep Jeffrey safe. He still blamed himself for not saving Jeffrey. Bud and I were very much alike, and he, too, used humor to get through catastrophic things.

Bud laughed, "Lynette was right. Jeffrey is kind of heavy."

While we waited at the gate for our flight, we continued to make the best of the situation. We talked about Jeffrey as if he were there with us, alive. We made sure we all knew where he was at for any given moment. God forbid, we did not want to lose his ashes on the way to Maui.

I said, "Who's got Jeffrey?"

Bud replied, "I do, but I'm going to the restroom. You watch him."

Kim said, "I'll carry him. Let's go look at the shops."

Marisol said, "I'll hold Jeffrey."

By the time we got on the plane, the people around us had caught on that Jeffrey was in the backpack. The whole thing was an experience I never want to relive. American society raises us to believe that we will bury our parents, and our children will bury us.

While we were on the plane, the conversations continued. The couple sitting across from us started to play along. Kim quickly learned their names were Katy and Dave. Kim talked to anybody and everybody. Kim reminded Bud and me of Melinda, who never met a stranger. Katy and Dave were quite fun.

We ran into Katy and Dave again on Maui and went out for lunch. When they saw us, they continued the game with us. Katy asked, "Who's got Jeffrey?"

We shared the story of Jeffrey and why we were in Maui.

**Funny Story**

Kim and I stayed friends with Dave and Katy for years. In July, they came to Bud's surprise birthday celebration at our home in Captain Island.

Later that year, they invited Kim and me to their home for New Year's Eve, 2001. What an experience that turned out to be. They had all the guests decorate balloons. At midnight, all the guests released them into the sky. Of course, I sent Jeffrey words of love. I told him how very much I missed him. I promised him I would try not to be so sad.

Dozens of the other guests were animators from Disney Studios. Their balloons were unbelievable. They drew characters recognizable from Disney cartoons. I wanted to keep them. I did not draw any pictures.

Bud and Jeffrey always said, "Mom, you can't even draw stick people right!"

That was true and has stayed a family joke to this day.

CHAPTER 35

# HONORING JEFFREY

As promised in the Huge Expensive Vacation, Kim, Marisol, and I signed up for surfing lessons. Neither of us had ever surfed before. Of course, Bud did not need a lesson as he was already a fantastic surfer after living in both Hawaii and Florida. Surprisingly, the three of us managed to get up on our boards and surf. The proof that I surfed for Jeffrey, *in his honor*, shows in the photo below.

*Kathy Surfing in Honor of Jeffrey*

Let me describe the process: Surfing involves paddling, paddling, and even more paddling. That process only gets you out to the waves. Then when the perfect wave comes, it is paddling, paddling, and even more paddling to catch the wave. Once you catch the wave, you need to do a quick pushup on a moving and unstable surface to get into the standing position.

If you manage to stand and balance, you are surfing. Congratulations!

Kim and I thought our arms were going to fall off. We both got up and surfed back to the shore. However, when we got back to shore, the instructor did not let us out of the water.

He said, "Okay, fantastic job. Go back out and do it again."

Surfing was exceedingly more difficult than it looked.

**Dreaded Day**

No parent should have to bury their child. It was just heartbreaking.

This quote explained it to me:

> *When you bury your parents, you lose your past.*
> *When you bury your spouse, you lose your present.*
> *When you bury your child, you lose your future.*
>
> *~Anonymous*

On May 26, we loaded up with Jeffrey's ashes and made the trip to the black sand beach. We left at 7:00 a.m. to avoid traffic and tour buses on the famous Road to Hana. We arrived at the black sand beach. The view was breathtaking, and the beach was empty.

We walked down the winding path to the beach below. The water was a stunning color of blue, exactly as I remembered it from the trip with Jeffrey and my mother. The day was extremely emotional for all of us. The reality and finality of the situation hit us all. It was unbelievable and unfathomable that we were there to lay Jeffrey to rest.

Kim and Marisol planned a little ceremony. We had bought a fresh Hawaiian flower lei on the way to the beach. Kim brought holy water from Saint Patrick's Cathedral in New York City. We found a beautiful spot in the corner of the bay where Jeffrey's ashes would wash up into a cave. The water was warm and tranquil. We waded into the bay and placed a flower lei in the water.

Although Jeffrey was not religious, Kim and Marisol, both raised in the Catholic religion, performed a little service. Bud and I opened the container of Jeffrey's ashes and poured them into the circle formed by the flower lei. Marisol sprinkled the holy water into the ashes as Kim said a wonderful prayer. Jeffrey had a great send-off.

The beautiful black sand beach that Melinda, Jeffrey, and I enjoyed that wonderful day three years before was now his eternal home. It was both heart wrenching and tranquil at the same time. It was a heavenly place for Jeffrey to be, but it was supposed to be me, not Jeffrey.

*Jeffrey's Eternal Home*

## Luau Time

Drained and in silence, we made the trip back to the condominium. We all cleaned up for dinner. We had reservations for another event in the Huge Expensive Vacation. We were off to a luau for Jeffrey, *in his honor*. One thing Jeffrey loved was a good buffet.

"There's no better buffet than a luau. The food is spectacular, and so are the smokin' hot girls," Jeffrey always said.

We enjoyed the food, the atmosphere, and the dancing. Jeffrey attended a dozen luaus growing up, including that trip with Melinda. He especially loved girls from the time he knew there was a difference between boys and girls. He really enjoyed watching the girls do the hula.

Surprisingly, the hula dancers picked Bud and Marisol to go on stage to learn the hula. It was nice to see them laugh instead of cry. Kim and I watched and laughed as they struggled with the steps of the dance.

I wished Jeffrey were there with us. It was adorable to watch the two of them smile, even if it was just for a moment. Guaranteed, Jeffrey would have teased Bud if he had seen his dancing routine.

"Bud, you can't dance. You think you can, but you can't, Dude!" Jeffrey always said.

**Harley Davidson Rides**

Next on the list for the Huge Expensive Vacation was to ride Harleys. Bud and I rented two Harley Davidson motorcycles. Bud and Marisol rode together, and Kim and I rode together. We cruised around the island for the day.

We rode up to the hill country and shared lunch at an old store that opened in 1849. The food was delicious, and shopping in the store was fun. Filled with local fare, the store held great souvenir finds. Bud got sunburned while riding the motorcycle and was not a happy camper at all. Kim continues to tell the story of Bud and his sunburn even today. She also tells the story of how different, yet the same, Bud and Jeffrey were.

We took the motorcycles back, cleaned up, and dressed in our fancy clothes, as Jeffrey called them.

**Jeffrey's Favorite Restaurant**

Before we got to Mama's Fish House, we stopped and watched the windsurfers on the North Shore, just like Jeffrey loved to do. When we lived in Hawaii, the three of us would go up to the North Shore of Oahu and watch the huge waves come into Sunset Beach. The waves were so big that the ground shook. The largest one we saw crested at forty-five feet. It was an unbelievable sight to see. The boys and I loved it.

*Mama's Fish House Maui*

Dinner was excellent. We enjoyed a great meal in honor of Jeffrey. He would have loved every minute of the Huge Expensive Vacation. If only Jeffrey were here with us. I just was not sure how my life would ever go back together again, without Jeffrey.

On our final day on Maui, we went over to the south shore, to the town of Makena. Jeffrey loved turtles, or *Hanu* in Hawaiian. These turtles can hold their breath for up to four hours, but typically come up and breathe air every few minutes. We swam with turtles. It was so cool. We snorkeled around and looked at the coral and all the colorful fish.

**Depression**

I slipped deeper into depression, no matter how much I tried to stay in the spirit of the Huge Expensive Vacation. I believed it should have been me that was dead, not Jeffrey. It was all wrong; it was so wrong.

What was I supposed to do for the rest of my life? Should I just stay in Hawaii with Jeffrey? I did not want to leave him alone. I knew he would forever be in my heart and soul, but it felt so wrong.

Jeffrey was truly an old soul from the day he was born. He kept me alive so many times during the turmoil of marriages, divorces, and failed relationships. His kindness and love gave me hope and showed me true love.

*Rest in peace, my little Jeffrey!*

Thankfully, the World brought Kim into my life before *They* took Jeffrey. Did the world know that I would not make it on my own? Kim was like Jeffrey in so many ways. Her kindness would have to keep me going until I could find that purpose for myself.

I did not want to leave Jeffrey alone in Hawaii. Kim and Bud would never understand my thinking, but a mother who has lost a child would understand exactly what I thought and felt.

## Headed Home or Not

We packed up and loaded the suitcases in the car. Funny, we gained a new suitcase. Somehow, that always happened when we went to Hawaii. The shopping was unbelievable, and we always found something special to bring home. Now, it was extra special things to remind us of Jeffrey.

We got to the airport, checked our baggage, and headed towards the gate. Next thing we knew, the police directed us out of the airport. Baffling, there was no explanation, they simply said to leave the airport.

Finally, an announcement came over a loudspeaker. "Everybody must evacuate the building," they said.

After half an hour, the police announced they needed to transport bomb dogs over from the island of Oahu. They informed us that it would take hours to clear the airport and suggested we find something to do for three or four hours. Everyone had to leave the airport property.

There were no buses or vehicles allowed into the airport, so we walked back to town and had lunch.

*Kim, Kathy, and Marisol Farewell Jeffrey Lunch*

Overall, it took the authorities six hours to clear the airport and get us on a plane. My theory was that Jeffrey wanted us to spend a little more time with him in Maui. I would have stayed forever.

We finally got on the plane and took off. The whole reality of the situation crashed down on me. It was like being back in my truck that fateful night when Kim called me and told me somebody murdered Jeffrey.

## Hysterics

*How can I leave my baby boy alone in Hawaii?* I asked myself. I knew in my head he really was not there, but in my heart, I would miss him forever. I started to cry—not the sniffle kind of cry—I balled hysterically. Once again, I could taste tears and snot.

The flight attendants noticed I was crying uncontrollably. They asked Kim, "Is everything okay?"

Kim explained the situation. The flight attendants returned with ten bottles of vodka. They must have felt that alcohol was the answer to my problems. It was genuinely nice of them to be concerned. Kim took the bottles and thanked them for their kindness. I had not had a drink of alcohol in over eight years, and this would not have been the right time to start.

Kim drank two bottles on the way home. We took the rest with us. Those bottles lasted Kim for years. She has always been a one-drink girl. Bud and Marisol were fast asleep, so they missed the whole event. They laughed when they saw all the bottles of vodka and heard the story.

The Next Day Came. Even worse, it was back in California.

CHAPTER 36

# THE PROSECUTOR

How ironic. As we placed Jeffrey in his final resting place in Maui, Hawaii, a message came to our phone from the prosecuting attorney in Fallen Meadow, Utah. I wanted just a little time for my mind to settle or come to peace. There was no getting used to Jeffrey being dead.

When we got home, there was a message for me to return a call to the prosecutor. Not thinking of the time, I told Kim to call him back.

Kim said, "Kathy, it's 2:00 a.m." Of course, she would have to call later when we woke up and when people got to work. With that, we all went to bed wondering what next.

Surprisingly, I did not have Kim make the call to the prosecutor. I decided to be *Mom* and make the call myself. This was strange, as I had not voluntarily talked on a phone other than to Kim or Bud since I learned of Jeffrey's death and the police fiasco. This felt official, so I slipped back into my trained officer mode.

The words my father always told me popped into my head. "Buck up! Make the damn call!" Torrance said.

"I am Jeffrey's mother. We missed your call. We were in Hawaii for a week, placing Jeffrey in his final resting place. We got home late last night."

The prosecutor introduced himself. He sounded like a nice man. He said, "I wanted to offer my condolences on the loss of your son, Jeffrey. I will be the one prosecuting Jack Ashe."

"Thank you. What do we need to do?"

He continued, "That is what I wanted to talk to you about. You may find this strange, and you probably won't be happy about it, but I've decided to offer Jack Ashe a plea bargain."

**What the Hell?**

Shocked, my mind raced. *What the freaking hell is this man thinking?* That animal Jack Ashe put a sawed-off shotgun on my baby's stomach and pulled the freaking trigger. If that was not murder, damn it, what the hell was?

I demanded, "Why? This was plain and simple murder! The police arrested him for murder. What kind of plea bargain?"

Remember, as an officer when Jeffrey was a small child, I sat in innumerable courtrooms. I was very aware of how unjust our criminal justice system could be. I witnessed thousands of plea bargains take place in those courtrooms and saw daily how people got away with unbelievable crimes. Oh, the stories I could tell.

He answered, "I am going to offer him manslaughter with use of a deadly weapon."

"Are you kidding? He murdered Jeffrey with a sawed-off shotgun. It was not an accident. Jeffrey was defenseless. Why the hell would you give him a break?"

The victim's family has no say in the matter in the state of Utah.

With sadness in his voice, he answered, "I am afraid that the witnesses are not good people either. I have two witnesses who both have records the same length of Jack Ashe's. That gives me two bad guys saying the third bad guy was the one who shot Jeffrey."

I was not aware of that information, but instantly the scene at the House of Murder popped into my head. I detected then, and still knew in my heart, that something smelled fishy about the whole story of Jeffrey's murder.

Those suspicions escalated when the police had us meet them at that house, and the man named Jackson tried desperately to get us all to believe that Jack Ashe was the murderer. This truly upset me. There was more to the story than we were getting from the detective.

I said, "Wow, Really? We met the man named Jackson. He told us Jack Ashe murdered Jeffrey. He seemed determined to make sure we knew it was Ashe who murdered Jeffrey. We did not know who Ashe was. We had no idea if we were talking to the murderer himself or what. The whole situation was crazy."

Shocked, the prosecutor said, "Wait a minute, you talked to Jackson?"

I laughed sarcastically. "Well, we had no choice," I replied.

"He is one scary guy. What do you mean, you had no choice?" The Prosecutor asked.

Finally, I saw an opportunity to complain about the trip to the House of Murder. I said, "Detective J made us meet him at the house where Jeffrey was murdered. It was inhumane, but that is another story. I was devastated and in shock. Jackson came right out of the garage, the scene of Jeffrey's murder. He introduced himself as Jeff's friend and told us that Jeff had been staying there. That was all news to me. Jeffrey never mentioned him or staying there. Then he told us an elaborate story that he wanted us to believe."

The prosecutor responded, "I can't believe you were at that house. I have no idea why the police would have taken you to that place."

I said, "We thought we were meeting the detective at the police station to pick up Jeffrey's car and belongings. Detective J. said the car was not evidence, so he had no reason to move it. Then, he rudely informed us that we needed to move the car because the people wanted it out of their garage. I told Detective J that they could have moved Jeffrey's car anywhere else in the world than the exact spot where somebody murdered my son. Detective J replied, 'Whatever.'"

"I agree that it is horrible to bring the family to the scene of the murder. I will address that with the detectives."

Whether he really talked to those two bonehead detectives, I do not know, but it made me feel a little better that he understood the torment it caused me. I asked, "Thanks, what would manslaughter with use of a deadly weapon get Jack Ashe in terms of prison time?"

"The charges each hold a maximum of ten years and a minimum of three years. Of course, I would strive for the maximum."

I acquiesced, "Something is better than nothing. Either way, Jeffrey will still be dead."

He explained, "That is why I want to offer him a plea bargain. I am afraid if one person out of twelve believes there is reasonable doubt that one of the other bad guys murdered Jeffrey, then Jack Ashe will walk free."

"That would not be good. I might have to do something serious," I replied.

He did not respond to that. "I hope he will take the plea bargain. I don't think you would be able to live with it if Jack Ashe walked free, and nobody answered for your son's murder," the prosecutor said.

"Do you believe Jack Ashe would walk free?" I asked.

"Yes," he admitted. "These guys are nasty people. I seriously doubt Jack Ashe will consider or accept the plea bargain, but I feel like I must offer it to him to get resolution for Jeffrey's murder. I know it should be murder, but there are just too many bad guys involved."

I thanked him for all he was doing. It was not an easy thing to swallow.

He concluded, "I will see Jack Ashe on Tuesday with his attorney. I'll let you know what I find out."

After I hung up the phone, I relayed the conversation to Bud and Kim. Neither was thrilled with the idea of a plea bargain. I explained, "He is doing what he believes to be the best opportunity for us to get some time served for Jeffrey's murder."

The wait was on to hear back from the prosecuting attorney. More questions raced through my mind. *What will the decision be? Will Jack Ashe take the plea bargain?* There were so many questions in my head already, why not add some more?

I still had doubt that Jack was the actual murderer, but the police were sure they had their man. If he did not take the plea-bargain, I wondered how I would be able to sit through a trial every day. How could I listen to this horrific story day after day?

**Decisions Made**

After unloading a truckload of groceries on Tuesday morning in Waterloo, Texas, I headed back to Fallen Meadow, Utah. On Wednesday morning, as I drove down another American highway, I was surprised when my phone rang. I noticed it was from the prosecuting attorney, so I quickly pulled my truck over onto the side of the road, set my four-way hazard lights, and answered the phone call.

Excitedly, he said, "Jack Ashe accepted the plea bargain."

The prosecutor was like a kid in a candy store. Angry that Jack Ashe would get away with murder, I had to accept at least he would go to prison for twenty years, or so I thought. The prosecutor continued, "I was so surprised that Jack Ashe took the plea. This is certainly better than him walking away free."

I replied, "Yes. I guess it is." I knew in my heart and mind that I would have to kill him myself if he walked free. Thank god, *They* were looking out for me and made Jack Ashe take that plea bargain.

"When we met, he had his attorney with him. They whispered together, then Jack Ashe agreed to the plea bargain. I was shocked! He didn't even ask for a lesser charge. He just took the plea." the prosecutor responded.

## My Opinion

I asked, "Don't you find that a little odd? Do you think somebody forced him to take the plea? Was he paid off or threatened? Maybe the people in charge would kill him, too, if he didn't take the plea? I've seen that happen before. There is way more to this story. I'll leave it at that, but somebody just got away with murder."

He answered, "We will never know that answer. I am happy he took the plea. This really will be easier for you. You will not have to sit in court and listen to this go on and on every day."

"Yes. That is a blessing. What happens next?"

## Pre-Sentencing Report

"I will order a pre-sentencing investigation report to be conducted. After that, I will set a sentencing hearing. You and your family members will be able to speak at the sentencing hearing."

Since I had sat in hundreds of courtrooms, I knew what a pre-sentencing report was. This report gathers all the history of the detained person, so the judge knows who they are. It also gives recommendations as to sentencing and other pertinent information about the case.

I asked, "Will I be able to say anything to Jack Ashe?"

"No, you are only allowed to speak to the judge. You can tell him how this crime has affected you and your family's lives. You cannot say terrible things about Jack Ashe. You cannot speak directly to him. If you cannot follow these rules, you will not be allowed to speak."

I snapped, "Wow, isn't that just fantastic? Jack Ashe has more rights than I do, and Jeffrey has no rights. Oh yes, that's right, Jeffrey's dead!"

Obviously, this man dealt with over-emotional, grieving parents regularly, as he did not even flinch. He continued with the conversation.

"Unfortunately, that is how the system is designed. There is nothing I can do about it. You can type a statement and bring it with you. You may also bring a photo of Jeffrey. Is there anybody else that will want to speak on Jeffrey's behalf?" the prosecutor asked.

"Yes, I am sure his brother, Bud, will want to speak. I have absolutely no idea about his father. The man had nothing to do with Jeffrey all his life, or Bud, but he showed up for Jeffrey's funeral. He saw Jeffrey twice in eighteen years. I can give you his number. We've been divorced for eighteen years." I replied.

He continued, "Okay, thanks. I'll let you know the date of the sentencing hearing. You will be compensated for your time and mileage."

"What? I do not need compensation for speaking on behalf of my son. All I have left of him are photographs and memories. I will be there whenever and wherever I can stand up for him. He was my precious baby," I said.

"I completely understand. That is just how the system works. Unfortunately, witnesses are not as cooperative and helpful as you are. That is why they offer monetary incentives to get them to appear," he replied.

"Wow, that's sad. I will be there for Jeffrey come hell or high water," I said.

"Yes, it is. I'll call you when I know more," the prosecutor said.

I thanked him for doing his best for Jeffrey. At least this man achieved a bit of retribution for Jeffrey's murder. I sat in my truck on the side of the road and cried tears of utter loss, anger, and disappointment out of my system. It was a tremendous relief to know I would not have to go to court every day and listen to all the proceedings.

When I stopped, I did not put my required triangles out behind the trailer. When a tractor-trailer was not moving on the side of the road for any length of time, the driver, required by law, put out emergency safety warning triangles. These devices warned other drivers that the vehicle broke down or stopped. Thankfully, no police came by and questioned me as to why I was sitting on the side of the road crying with my four-way flashers on. They could have given me a ticket for that.

## Relay the Message

The last few months had been mindboggling. Never in my wildest dreams could I have imagined the things that had happened in my life. I was tired physically and drained emotionally. While I sat there contemplating the chaotic disaster my life became, I called Kim and relayed all the information to her and Bud.

Bud said, "Of course, I intend to speak at the sentencing hearing."

I replied, "You need to know there are strict rules you must follow. You cannot say anything to Jack Ashe, and you cannot punch him in the face."

Bud laughed, "Well, that would certainly make me feel better, but I will follow whatever rules there are, as long as I get to tell my side of the story for Jeffrey."

"The prosecutor will call your father and tell him what happened and see if he wants to talk at the sentencing hearing."

Bud replied, "Okay, I would assume he would want to be there."

"Bud, I have no idea. Who knows, I never thought he would show up in your life again. I wouldn't even try to guess what he and Gail are thinking. Love you, Bud!" I said.

"Love you, too, Mom!" Bud replied.

I blew my nose, dried my eyes, and put on my blinker to get back on the highway. I needed to get back to Fallen Meadow. I wanted to get home to my little family in Captain Island and write my statement.

## CHAPTER 37

# SENTENCED, SO WHAT?

The sentencing hearing was set for June 26. What was the world trying to tell me? Was the number 26 a mysterious message from Jeffrey? He died on March 26, we bought tickets for Hawaii on April 26, we laid Jeffrey to rest in Maui on May 26, and now the sentencing hearing was June 26. How long would this cycle continue?

Once again, Bud, Kim, Marisol, and I planned a trip to Fallen Meadow. First, we started up our computers and began to write statements we would make at the hearing. This was certainly not a painless process. We shed hundreds of tears as we tried to put in mere words what Jeffrey meant to our family and to each of us individually. There were not enough words in the English language to put all that on one sheet of paper.

Choosing Jeffrey's photo for the sentencing hearing was even more important for us. We were on a mission to make sure the judge understood how important Jeffrey was to us. He needed to understand how very much we missed him and how our lives would never be the same again without him. Our main goal was to influence the judge to inflict on Jack Ashe the harshest sentence possible. If we had our way, he would never get out of prison.

I explained to my work I would not be available for the trip the following week as I had a sentencing hearing to attend. We drove to Fallen Meadow on Sunday and spent a couple of days at Lynette's home before the hearing.

Marisol had never heard the story of my days as an officer in Fallen Meadows. I said, "It's ironic that years ago when Jeffrey was a toddler,

I took detainees from that very jail where Jack Ashe is being held to the same courthouses where we will speak about Jeffrey's murder. I remember the endless hours I sat in those courtrooms listening to people get away with crime after crime. The stories I could tell you."

Marisol said, "Are you kidding me?"

"Now, I am going there for the sentencing of the man that murdered my son, and he too, will get away with murder."

To me, this was the definition of absurdity. It was going to be a long and torturous day for all of us. I did not know how we could sit in the courtroom with the man who supposedly murdered Jeffrey.

## Family Representation

Jeffrey's family filled the courtroom for the sentencing hearing. Present were Kim, Bud, Marisol, me, Lynette, and her children, along with their families. Friends of Jeffrey were there and people I did not even know. We believed that the greater the number of people in attendance, the greater the impact would be on the judge; he could see the number of lives Jeffrey affected.

Even Artie and Gail showed up. Although Artie attended the hearing, he would not read a statement. He told the prosecuting attorney he could not follow the guidelines the court set forward.

Artie said, "I have plenty of things to say to the asshole who murdered my son."

## Sentencing Statement

I read my statement as I held an eleven-by-fourteen photo of Jeffrey. There was not a dry eye in the courtroom when I finished. Even the judge asked for a tissue.

> Your Honor:
>
> This is my son, Jeffrey, murdered at eighteen years of age. This is all I have left—photographs and memories. I would like to tell

you about Jeffrey so you can understand the loss and devastation this has caused my family, especially me.

Jeffrey was the best-behaved, loving, and most affectionate baby I have ever known. He always shared kisses and hugs. As he grew older, he always had an *I love you* or *It will be all right* when times were tough. Jeffrey loved life; he was easy going and laid back. He always had a smile or a laugh.

Jeffrey had the deepest voice. Girls used to ask him questions, just so he would talk, and they could hear his voice. He was always willing to help people out. He would drive miles out of his way to give rides to people. Believe me. I have the mileage on my cars.

Jeffrey loved children and animals, especially poodles. He always talked about having a son of his own to raise and love. He imagined all the things they would do together. Now, that will never happen. We will never see Jeffrey get married or have children.

At the age of five, a psychiatrist diagnosed Jeffrey with acute dyslexia and evaluated his IQ at 163, which is in the genius range. He not only reversed numbers and letters, but he reversed syllables and wrote words completely backward. He learned in a completely unique way.

It was quite a struggle both financially and emotionally for Jeffrey, me, and my other son, Bud, who will also speak today. As a single parent, with no aid from their father, the state, or government, I spent more than $100,000 to provide Jeffrey with private specialized school and medical treatment for him to be able to read, write, and do math.

Though it was not an easy road to travel, Jeffrey not only graduated from high school with a 3.195 GPA, but he just graduated from heating and air conditioning school in January of this year, first in his class. He chose this career because he would be able to take those skills anywhere and had the potential to support himself and his family.

Jeffrey loved the water. He won dozens of trophies and awards for swimming. With his love of the water, Jeffrey became a Red Cross certified lifeguard and a certified scuba diver. He also loved to surf.

Jeffrey loved tropical islands. We traveled together to Hawaii, Tahiti, and the Grand Cayman Islands. Jeffrey was my traveling partner. Recently, sadly, we took his ashes and laid him to rest on the black sand beach he loved in Maui, Hawaii.

Jeffrey waited his entire life to be eighteen and an adult. He finally made it, and then Jack Ashe took it all away. None of this story will bring Jeffrey back to life, but I hope it will help you to see the incredibly special person Jack Ashe took from us. We will never see him become the man I know in my heart he would have been. I will have a hole in my heart for the rest of my life.

I hope and pray that someday Jack Ashe will understand what he has done and change his life to a future without drugs and violence. Let him never hurt another human being again. I know that is what Jeffrey would have wanted. I hope and pray that you, Your Honor, will give Jack Ashe the maximum sentence possible, so that he will have an enormous amount of time to think about what he has done and who he has taken away.

Thank you!

Bud read his statement after mine. It took coaching and extreme restraint for him to walk past Jack Ashe. He wanted so badly to take revenge for Jeffrey. I explained to Bud that it would only get him in trouble. It would have absolutely no effect on Jack Ashe or his sentence.

Bud, in unbelievable pain, gave his speech. He not only lost his brother; he also lost his best friend. His life turned upside down and inside out. I could not have been prouder of Bud. He had become a man of integrity with rigorous standards. I hoped I had a part in making him this man, along with the U.S. Navy. Bud stood for Jeffrey with dignity and strength.

## Sentenced

The judge sentenced Jack Ashe to the maximum he could within the parameters of the law. He sentenced him to ten years for manslaughter with use of a deadly weapon. Jack Ashe would serve at least four years of those ten before he was eligible for parole on that charge.

The judge sentenced Jack Ashe to ten years for robbery with use of a deadly weapon. After receiving parole on the first charge, he would serve at least four years of those additional ten years on the robbery charge before he would be eligible for parole on that charge.

Sentenced to a total of twenty-years, Jack Ashe would have to serve a minimum of eight years and a maximum of twenty for both charges. To me, this sentence was disgusting at best, but I know by the tears the judge shed that he did the best he could within the laws of the state of Utah.

We have such an unjust justice system in America. This sentence in no way compensated for the life Jack Ashe took from my family and me. There was no closure for my family on this day of sentencing for Jack Ashe. I planned to attend every parole hearing for which Jack Ashe became eligible. No matter where I was, I would be there to stand for Jeffrey.

I would ensure Jack Ashe served every single day possible on his sentence. I swore to Jeffrey that for as long as I was alive and able to get there, I would be his voice. There would never be enough time for Jack Ashe to serve.

## Mothers Meet

After the sentencing hearing, as we walked out of the courtroom and into the hallway, an extremely odd thing happened. A woman walked up to me, obviously terribly upset, and crying. I had no idea who she was or why she approached me. When she was able to gather herself, she said something to me that totally shocked me.

She said, "I am Jack Ashe's mother. I am so deeply sorry. I can't believe what happened. Poor Jeffrey. I met him. He was such a sweet boy. I don't understand. I am so very deeply sorry."

I never even imagined or even thought about the animal that murdered my child having a mother. I was surprised that this strange, crying woman spoke to me. I was not surprised that she could not complete a sentence after I realized who she was. She was highly upset. I didn't know what to say to this woman.

I was even more shocked that she had met Jeffrey. *What?* How had Jack Ashe's mother met Jeffrey? This was unbelievable; I knew there was more to this story. My grandmother's raising me to have manners always came back to me, even in the most painful, bizarre situations. This time, it came back and bit me right in the ass.

I replied, "Thank you."

"I can't believe I gave birth to a murderer," she said.

This woman was obviously distraught and suffering from this knowledge. I had no idea Jack Ashe had anybody in the courtroom who was his family. I had so much pain and anger in me, but I understood that this woman hurt too. I was sure she tried her best to raise a decent human being and realized this very day, with the finality of the sentencing, that she had failed.

I tried to be compassionate. It was not easy under the circumstances. "I am sorry too. The difference is that you have twenty years to hope your son can become a better person. My son will still be dead."

She said, "I know. I hope he will get his life straightened out this time."

The words, *this time,* threw me over the edge. I could not be civil any longer. Calmly I said, "Thanks. I have to go now."

I know, as a mother, this woman was suffering, but I had nothing left to give to anyone. My world was torn into bits and pieces, shattered.

**The Truth**

No matter what I did, no matter what anybody said, my son Jeffrey would never come back to life. I would never see or talk to him again. I would never hear his deep voice again, nor his laughter or singing in the shower. Most sadly, I would never hear him say *I love you* again.

At this point, I would have been happy to hear Jeffrey say, *I s'pose I'm in trouble*. The little baby I held in my arms was gone. All the struggles, time, and effort to help him grow into an adult had been for what?

A man had just gotten away with murder. Jack Ashe plea-bargained his time into years he would not have to serve. I knew from experience he would earn time off for so many things. Prisoners earn good time, work time, school time, I-am-an-asshole time, and a never-ending list of times taken off their sentences.

It was so unfair. Jeffrey was dead. What about all the time Jack Ashe took from Jeffrey's life? What about what he did to Bud's life, my life? How does an animal put a sawed-off shotgun on the stomach of an eighteen-year-old young boy and blow him away? What did Jack Ashe really get for the life of my child? We will never know, but I still to this day believe there was more to the story.

Jack Ashe never apologized to me for murdering Jeffrey. He showed no concern, guilt, or remorse for what he had done.

Bud and I would never be the same. We would figure out how to live our lives without Jeffrey. The Three Musketeers became Two of a Kind.

CHAPTER 38

# LOVE STORIES AND BACKSTABS

Heartbroken and lost, Bud and I walked out of the courthouse. There would always be an empty spot in our hearts and souls. People and relationships had come and gone in our lives, but one thing had always remained consistent—we had each other. It was something on which the three of us always depended.

The experience in the courtroom was unbelievably draining—to speak, cry, and tell a courtroom full of people the horror and pain of losing a child to murder. Bud and I poured our hearts out to the judge.

We needed to come down from all the stress and drama of the courthouse. The group decided to have lunch. Since Artie and Gail were there, I invited them to join us for lunch. We went out to the Steak Corral, a favorite of Jeffrey and Bud's as they were growing up. Believe me, they did not make money on the $4.99 all-you-can-eat buffet when these two boys were in the restaurant.

To honor Jeffrey, we decided to eat at the buffet. Nobody was in the mood to eat, but we did the best we could. The six of us sat and talked about the sentencing hearing. Bud and I were still shaking from our experience of speaking.

It was impossible to describe the value and loss of your loved one in a court of law. Pray it never happens to you and your family. We discussed all the people who had shown up. Family and friends represented Jeffrey well. We were all thankful the judge understood our loss and sentenced Jack Ashe to the longest sentence he could.

Something that shocked all of us was that Jack Ashe had nothing to say for himself. He showed zero remorse for what he had done to Jeffrey or our family. He was smug and arrogant. In fact, it appeared that he was proud that he murdered somebody.

The judge asked Jack Ashe, "What did you do?"

Jack Ashe said flatly, "I put a sawed-off shotgun on Jeff's stomach and pulled the trigger."

There was nothing on his face. His eyes were empty. It made me so angry. It took everything I had to stay in my seat and not say anything. To us, he was an inhuman animal. It was heartbreaking to all of us, especially Bud and me.

We needed to change the subject, so to interrupt the disgust with what happened in the courtroom, we started to tell Jeffrey stories. Thankfully, Bud and I knew endless stories to tell about Jeffrey.

**Jeffrey Story**

When the boys were growing up and we came to eat at the Steak Corral, the boys would finish eating, and Jeffrey knew he could go play video games in the arcade room. With his IQ of 163, it took him no time at all before he could beat any video game.

A couple of his favorites were the pinball machines and the race car game. One of the stories of the Steak Corral I will never forget was when the video game Mortal Combat came out, and they added it to the arcade room at the restaurant.

Jeffrey went to play video games. When I finished eating, I went to the recreation room door and yelled for Jeffrey so he could hear me over the noise of the games.

I shouted, "Jeffrey, hurry up and die—we have to go!"

After Jack Ashe murdered Jeffrey, I wondered if I set up the forces of the Universe to make Jeffrey's murder happen. I felt guilty about that, even as I was telling the story.

We said our farewell to Artie and Gail. This time, I knew it would be for the last time. They headed back to Wisconsin. Like a bad penny, they just kept showing up. Their appearance had no purpose to me other than them being at the sentencing hearing gave the judge the appearance that Jeffrey had an even bigger family that loved him.

I hoped that after the death of Jeffrey, Bud's father could find it in his heart to build a relationship with Bud, as he was struggling with the loss of Jeffrey. The damage Artie and Gail did to my children and me back in 1982 no longer held meaning to me.

Artie's and Gail's betrayals were so minor in comparison to what Jack Ashe did to Bud and me. Years ago, we survived losing their father and my husband. Bud and I would figure out a way to survive the loss of Jeffrey, together.

**Jeffrey's Car Goes Home**

Before we left California for the sentencing hearing, Bud and I decided to pick up Jeffrey's car and bring it home. Jeffrey's car had sat at my work for three months. Bud felt the car should be drivable. If not, he would be able to fix it, or we could get it towed.

A funny thing happened when we went to my work to pick up Jeffrey's car. There was a large black bird sitting on the fence in front of Jeffrey's car. When we got out of our car, the black bird did not fly away. It started to caw and make a sweet gurgling sound while looking at us.

I said, "Do you think that black bird is Jeffrey? I know it's been a long day, but the bird appears to be trying to tell us something."

Bud replied, "I don't know Mom, but he doesn't seem to be afraid of us at all."

"Kathy, that thought is so heart-felt, it has to be Jeffrey. The bird is not leaving; he's telling you a story." Kim replied.

"Hello, Jeffrey. Thank you for coming to see us. The sentencing is over, and we're taking your car home with us. I hope that is okay. Jeffrey, I love you and miss you so much," I said as I doubled over in tears.

"Yea, Jeffrey, me too," said Bud.

Marisol said, "Kathy, what a beautiful loving gift. Thank you, Jeffrey."

"Jeffrey always wanted to be a bird. He used to ask me why he wasn't born one," I said. It was strange that thought came into my mind right at that very moment.

The large black bird cawed a couple more times and flew away. I do not know if the bird was Jeffrey or not, but it sure gave us comfort at an exceedingly difficult moment in our lives. From that day, I have seen mostly black birds, but a variety of birds that come and talk to me until I share an *I Love You and Miss You*, then the bird flies away.

Bud and Marisol got into Jeffrey's car and it started right up. Kim and I followed Bud in case anything broke down. We were members of AAA and would be able to call for a tow truck to take it to a repair shop if necessary. Bud gave it a thorough go-over before we hit the highway. We stopped at the nearest gas station to fill it up with gas. Bud checked all the vital fluids and put air in the silly looking tires.

With two vehicles, we headed off to California. The trip was successful, and we made it back to Captain Island without incident. We parked the awful looking car with its primer paint job and its funny wheels and tires in the parking lot of our upscale townhouse.

It was not long before the neighbors started asking questions about the car. Those comments stopped instantly when people found out the car belonged to my murdered son. However, Kim and I knew they were not thrilled with the awful-looking car sitting in the parking lot.

Kim and I decided to rearrange things in the garage and put the car inside. This made the neighbors and us happy. Besides, it would be easier for us to work on the car inside the garage.

**Geo Prizm Restoration**

Kim, Bud, Marisol, and I are, I am sure, the only people in history to restore a 1993 Geo Prizm. It took us quite a while. The car had over 250,000 miles on it, but that did not matter to us. The most important thing about this car was that it belonged to Jeffrey.

Eighteen-year-old boys do not have possessions. Jeffrey had this vehicle and he loved it; therefore, we loved it. The restoration took dozens of trips to junkyards in California. Bud designed a plan to restore the car, and we followed it.

The seats were re-upholstered in a shop Bud and Marisol found. The last thing we did was to have it painted to cover over that god-awful primer. Bud found a shop that painted it for $700. We decided to paint it black, as that was the color of mourning, and we were mourning.

That stereo that Jeffrey put in the car, the one that cost me $1,500 to get back from the city of Bighorn, was something else. The trunk was full of speakers and amplifiers that made the car *thump* with sound.

Music made me cry, so I did not listen to it very often. I usually listened to audio books, only murder and mystery stories. That stereo took audiobooks into a whole new story adventure.

*Jeffrey's Geo Prizm Restored*

**Funny Jeffrey Car Story**

One night, I drove Jeffrey's car down the highway. The stereo was thumping with the Eagles; I was playing the only music I listened to. Next thing I knew, the local police pulled me over. The officer walked up to the car window. When I rolled the window down, he was shocked. He saw me, a mature lady, driving the car that was thumping on his roadway, and he laughed aloud.

He said, "Have a nice evening, Ma'am!"

I am sure a juvenile would not have gotten off so easily.

The car turned out beautifully. Bud and I drove it for years. Restoring Jeffrey's car was good therapy for us all. We spent hours together. As we worked on the car, we talked about Jeffrey and wondered about his life.

We never did find out why Jeffrey covered the car in primer or why he put those god-awful wheels and tires on the car. We will never know what happened in Fallen Meadows, but in our hearts, we at least knew that Jeffrey was at peace.

**The Death of Jeffrey's Car**

The sad ending to the story of Jeffrey's car came in June of 2010 when a longtime family friend convinced me to give Jeffrey's car to their son to use while they attended college in Nebraska to become a psychiatrist. They said that he needed a vehicle to drive back and forth to school.

"Since you really don't use Jeffrey's car, can you lend it to him to use while in school? I know he would cherish it as much as you do, since it's Jeffrey's car. You know he loved Jeffrey."

I fell for the story, *hook, line, and sinker*, as the saying goes. I shipped the car to Nebraska, with one truly clear understanding. If he did not want Jeffrey's car for any reason, he was to call me, and I would ship Jeffrey's car back home to me, no expense to him.

I found out from his brother, that he had a different plan figured out before I even shipped Jeffrey's car. When the car arrived, he drove it like a race car. He took part in an activity the kids called *drifting*, driving at a high rate of speed and pulling the hand brake inside the car, forcing the car to skid.

Remember, this was a 1993 Geo Prizm. First, it was not designed for this kind of treatment, and secondly, it already had over 250,000 miles of wear and tear on it. Well, it did not take long, and he literally broke the brake handle off inside the car and god knows what else.

With no regard for his solemn promise to call me, the little creep traded Jeffrey's car in on a pickup truck for himself.

He did not have balls enough to call me or return Jeffrey's car as promised. He never told me he did not want Jeffrey's car, nor that he broke it. If only he would have told me that I needed to ship Jeffrey's car back to my home! Unbelievably, I lost Jeffrey's car forever.

**An Ass Is an Ass Is an Ass**

Furthermore, that little creep never apologized to me for the heartache and pain he caused me. I called and confronted him; he was a smart ass.

"You need to get over it and move on. It was just a car." He snapped.

"You ass, you better pray you never lose your child!" I snapped back.

The little snake yelled and blamed me on the phone. He was an ass, to say the least. He hung up on me and has never apologized. We have not spoken since that call and never will. People sure are something else, aren't they?

That car was part of Jeffrey that I can never replace. It might have just been a car, as he so nastily put it to me, but it was the car of my dead child, whom I can never replace. I tried to find out where the car was and if I could get it back, but it was gone. The last thing I had of Jeffrey was forever senselessly lost, just like Jeffrey.

Eighteen-year-old boys do not have things. Jack Ashe stole the few other things Jeffrey had. Anything else left was still in police evidence.

**One Last Slap in the Face**

We eventually received the things from police evidence. I cannot remember when or how, but I distinctly remembered that they came in Ziploc bags. Yes, plastic bags. They even sent his clothing covered in blood and feces.

It was unbelievable and oh so painful. To this day, I have no comprehension or understanding of the lack of empathy in the police departments involved in the life of Jeffrey. There are no words to describe the pain these unnecessary events caused me.

The few things I kept are still in the same Ziploc bags. I have no idea what to do with them. I look at them occasionally when I move or sort through things, but they just make me cry.

*Authors Note:* The little creep never became a psychiatrist.

CHAPTER 39

# BIRTHDAYS WITHOUT JEFFREY

Bud struggled with guilt for not saving Jeffrey. I tried to be strong and help him. Bud believed that had he stopped in Fallen Meadow when he moved to California earlier that year and brought Jeffrey to California, Jeffrey would still be alive. In his heart, Bud needed to save his brother.

Bud played *would have, could have,* and *should have* games, just like me. It would not get him anywhere. I knew that and he knew that, but this was what we did in our heads. Our brains tried to fix things and convince us that dreadful things had not happened to our family. Those things only happened on television.

I talked to Bud every day. I told him he needed to do things to make Jeffrey proud—he should go to school and become the man Jeffrey believed him to be. Bud worked hard in the Navy and got every promotion he could.

Bud did all the things Jeffrey could no longer do—he surfed, danced, learned to scuba dive, and loved children and poodles. However, a huge red flag arose when Bud did not want to celebrate his birthday. He did not have Jeffrey to share it with, so he was not interested in having his birthday. July 17 would never be the same birthday for Bud or for me.

My brain went around and around with this birthday situation. I tried to figure out how to help Bud.

Kim suggested, "Let's have a birthday week for Bud."

"Great idea, Kim. That sounds like fun."

"Kathy, we can have a surprise party at our townhouse and invite all our friends and Marisol's family. We can give Bud birthday presents every day."

Mostly, we gave Bud mechanical tools to work on his cars and guy stuff. We did our best to let him celebrate his own birthday as he would never have Jeffrey to celebrate with him again.

Nobody, not even Kim or Bud, recognized or acknowledged that I lost my child, and it would have been his 19th birthday. The day was all about Bud and his feelings, his loss, which was okay, I guess. Inside, I was devastated and broken-hearted; I had lost my baby. It was so hard to keep being the strong one, the fixer, the one who took care of everyone.

I guess I was helping Bud at a great cost to myself.

**Survivor's Guilt**

Bud suffered from survivors' guilt. He needed to know it was okay to still be alive. Because he was in the military, he could not seek professional help as that would appear on his military record. He felt it would prevent him from receiving promotions in the future.

An incident happened one weekend when Bud walked across the street to a local bar. He obviously had way too much to drink. Kim and I heard him out front of our house by the babbling creek, yelling and mumbling to himself.

Bud said, "It was all my fault, I should have done something. I knew those people were bad."

I asked, "What people, Bud?"

He just mumbled more. Kim and I brought him into the house. He was so upset about Jeffrey. He kept saying it was his fault that Jeffrey died. I never did find out what Bud thought he knew about *those people*, but it continued to confirm my belief that there was more to the murder of Jeffrey than I was ever made aware of.

We got Bud into bed. Somehow, we needed to convince him that it was not his fault. What a mess—Jeffrey's death was my fault, and Bud believed it was his. How were two people, both thinking they were guilty, ever going to make it through?

Too bad Jack Ashe did not believe it was his fault.

I was not even sure why I remained alive myself. My thinking was not in a particularly good place at all.

The Next Day Came. The days just kept on coming.

CHAPTER 40

# LIFE GOES ON

*The Next Day* would not stop coming. I tried to do the next thing and be strong. Kim dropped me off at Poison Oak International Airport—back to another week of work, another flight to Fallen Meadow, Utah. It should have been clear to somebody I should not be driving 80,000 pounds of steel truck down a highway. Yet, I continued to go to work.

What was I supposed to do next? I had no idea, but I needed to figure it out quickly. My brain was not thinking good thoughts. Spending days by myself was not a good thing; I had too much time to think and play mind games. Once again, I occupied my mind with questions. My biggest question was: *What is my purpose now?*

I returned to my normal run of delivering industrial groceries from Fallen Meadow, Utah, to Rancho Santiago, California. Things seemed to be back into a routine, but I wondered how the week would go with a trip to California again. I left Rancho Santiago around 10:00 a.m. and headed north out of California to Fallen Meadow.

It was Thursday, July 26, 2001. Another 26 in the crazy pattern of things in my life. It was my last trip back to Fallen Meadow for the week. I made valuable time out of California as traffic was light for a change. My goal was to get to the distribution center, park my truck, and get to the airport in time for my flight to Poison Oak.

I came down the mountain pass and rolled across the California-Utah state line. In Utah, the speed limit went up to 75 mph. I set my cruise control and looked forward to getting back to the distribution center, the airport, and food before my flight.

I said aloud, "Wow, I haven't even had a flat tire this week."

**Jeffrey's Words of Wisdom**

*What was I thinking?*

Jeffrey always said, "Mom, don't say those kinds of things aloud. Don't even think them; you'll curse yourself! Really Mom, listen, when you say things like stay out of trouble or make sure you get home on time, you always curse me."

I told him, "Jeffrey, I do not have the power to put curses on people. I do not have power over the Universe."

"Seriously, Mom, you make that very thing happen," Jeffrey had said.

BANG! There was a huge explosion. My truck shook violently. It took a split second for my mind to register what happened. I said aloud, "Holy f**k, I blew a front tire!"

**Flat Tire from Hell**

I realized at that moment that I had spent an inordinate amount of time talking to myself since the murder of Jeffrey. "Pay attention Kathy, this is not a good thing," I shouted aloud.

The flat was on the passenger side of the tractor and pulling my truck hard towards the right shoulder of the highway. I knew if I did not hold onto the steering wheel and keep the truck going straight, the whole thing would go off the road and into the desert.

*Holy crap Batman!* This was every driver's nightmare. Thankfully, my thoughts were rational, or were they? Everything happened in a split second, but in slow motion. That dysfunctional, functioning personality flipped on in less than a heartbeat.

Everything I had ever learned about blowing a front tire came into my brain. I knew exactly what to do and what not to do. I knew not to slam on the brakes as this could cause the truck to flip. I calmly turned off the cruise control as this stopped the fuel from going to the engine.

Weighing in at 120 pounds, I stood up and held the steering wheel to the left as the truck shook violently. It took every bit of strength I had to keep the truck going in a straight line. My life flashed before my eyes in an instant.

The thought entered my mind: *If I want to live, I better keep the truck on the road surface.* I knew if the tractor went off the pavement, it would suck the truck, the trailer, and me into the desert. The tractor and trailer would undoubtedly flip over and roll, and I would end up in a mangled mess.

My irrational head said: *You could let go of the wheel, and all the suffering would be over.*

My rational head said: *What if you hurt somebody else? What if you do not die? What if you end up even more miserable?*

"Focus!" I shouted.

My heart raced a hundred miles an hour. The tractor vibrated like a wild and crazy carnival ride. My brain kicked into remote control, and I did the things necessary to stay alive. The vehicle finally slowed down enough for me to pull the truck to the side of the road and stop. I sat down and pulled the air brakes.

## Messages

Karma, the Universe, or whoever tried desperately to send me a message. The tractor might have stopped vibrating, but I shook like a leaf in a Florida hurricane.

"Are you freaking kidding me? What now?" I shouted to the sky.

*Oh my god!* I had driven over one million accident and ticket free miles across this country through all sorts of weather. I had never blown a front tire before. There were two things in my favor. First, my trailer was empty—that made it easier to control the vehicle and slow it down to a stop quicker. Second, I had not panicked.

I was only forty miles from the distribution center in Fallen Meadow. I wanted to go home. Now, parked on the side of the interstate, once again with another flat tire, I took a deep breath and closed my eyes for a moment.

Unbelievably, Jeffrey was correct. I could curse people, even myself.

*Thank you, Jeffrey, for keeping me safe.* I knew in my heart he was indeed now my Guardian Angel. He was laughing for sure, especially on this day when I cursed myself with my flat tire statement. Whatever the message was, it cost me time and money. Driving a tractor-trailer for a living, I quickly learned unless the wheels were turning, I was not making any money.

Once I was breathing again, I got out of my tractor, dug around in the side toolbox, and found my emergency triangle markers. I carefully worked my way to the back of the trailer. There were vehicles, including tractor-trailers, flying by me at over 75 mph. This caused tremendous wind gusts and suction at the same time. I put a triangle on the road at 50 feet, 100 feet, and 200 feet distances.

Once again, I called my company to get a flat tire fixed. It was funny how quickly we came to rely on cell phones. In trucking, they were truly a blessing. When I first started truck driving, there was no such thing as a pager, cell phone, or GPS. I traveled through all forty-eight states with an extra-large laminated map book and a citizen's band (CB) radio.

All I wanted to do was get to the terminal, back my trailer into the door, turn in my paperwork, and head for the airport. Nope, that was not going to happen. I would be sitting there for a couple of hours at least.

**Better Call Kim**

*Just what I need, more time to sit on the side of a highway and contemplate how my life went to hell. Will this ever stop? Will I even be able to catch the last flight to Poison Oak?*

I decided I had better call Kim and let her know what happened this time. I said casually, "Hey, guess what? I blew another tire." I relayed the above story to her in graphic details.

She said, "Are you kidding me? Are you okay? You scare the crap out of me."

"Yes, I am fine. It was quite a ride, though."

Kim said, "Thank god, you are alive. I do not know what I would do without you. Are they coming to fix the tire?"

"Yes, they are on the way, but who knows how long that will take. I will not make the early flight. Will you change the flight for me?"

"Okay, let me know when you are up and running again," she replied.

"I will. I just want to get home and hang out with you and Bud for the weekend."

It took hours for the technician to come to me on the interstate and change the tire. I signed all the paperwork, picked up my emergency triangles, and put them away in the tractor toolbox. I started up my truck and headed for the distribution center.

Things went well the rest of the way to the distribution center. I got into the yard, opened the trailer doors, backed the trailer into door sixteen, and went inside.

**Will This Day Ever End?**

The terminal manager met me at the door. He did not look happy, and I knew I was not going to be happy either.

He said, "You need to unhook your tractor and park it over on the west side of the lot for the weekend. They are going to do maintenance on all the tractors."

I growled, "I hope I don't miss my flight."

The trailer connects to the tractor by the kingpin, a five-inch by two-inch round pin that comes down from the trailer. This pin slides into the fifth wheel device, a big black greasy apparatus, on the tractor which locks and holds the kingpin on the trailer to the tractor.

The process of unhooking the tractor from the trailer:

1. The driver chocks the tires of the trailer with a little triangular block placed in front of the trailer tires that keeps the trailer from moving when the truck pulls out from under the trailer.
2. The driver unhooks the power connectors and air hoses found on the front of the trailer and back of the tractor. These supply lights to the trailer and air to the air brake system on the trailer.
3. The driver lowers the landing gear that holds the trailer up when the tractor pulls out from under the trailer. The driver turns a

handle counterclockwise and lowers the two legs with platforms on the bottom.

4. With the trailer secured, on the driver side of the tractor, the driver reaches over the dual tires on the tractor and under the trailer to reach the kingpin lever. Clearance is less than eight inches. With a fully extended arm, the driver grabs the release lever handle and gives it a big jerk to make the kingpin release.

5. When the kingpin releases, the driver gently pulls the tractor out from under the trailer and can then drive the tractor separately.

I completed the above procedure, and all went well until the big jerk. I gave the kingpin release a big jerk, and nothing happened. This pissed me off. It had already been a horrible day. Was it not enough for one day? I gave it an even bigger jerk.

*Bam!* The kingpin released, but something went wrong, terribly wrong. *Oh my god!* Fiery pain went up my arm, into my neck, and down my back.

**The Hell Continued**

Once again, I could not breathe or move. It was just un-freaking believable. It was July and hotter than hell. I was mentally and physically exhausted. I hung over the hot, dirty, dual tires in unbearable pain.

Slowly, I moved out from under the trailer and cried. Somehow, I got my arm down to my side and even managed to stand upright. What had I done? Hurt and angry, I climbed back up into the tractor, drove it to the side, and parked it.

I grabbed my bag, carefully climbed out, slammed the door, and swore. I walked back up to the terminal to report my injury. I needed to fill out an injury report. I wondered if I could even make a flight back to California.

I went to the door, gave it a pull with my good arm, and it did not budge. The door would not move. Really!

**Injured and Alone**

Everybody had gone home and left me there alone. Exasperated, I sat down and cried. How could everybody get into their vehicles, go home, and leave me at the distribution center alone? They wanted to get home to their family and dinner. Whatever, I wanted to go home too.

My next question was how I would get to the airport. I could barely turn my neck left to right or up and down. There was no way I could drive a motorcycle with one arm to the airport. One way or the other, I was going home.

I called a taxi to take me to the airport. There was nothing else to do but wait. There was no way I was going to an emergency room for hours by myself. I sat on the steps and cried some more. I was tired of being alone. I just wanted to go home.

The struggle had beaten me down. I truly had no idea how I would manage. The journey alone I had undertaken as a single parent proved to be a huge challenge. The responsibility, at times, was overwhelming. Somehow, I endured long enough to get my sons grown, only to have an animal murder one of them. This alone took the fight out of me. It just would not stop.

As I sat there alone, injured, having just survived a life-threatening, near-death experience, I did not know if I could take anymore. I looked up at the now dark sky.

I shouted, "I am mentally exhausted and now physically hurt, what else do you want from me? Can't you take me home too, so I can be with Jeffrey?"

Nobody answered, nobody ever answered.

## Another Call to Kim

I called Kim and told her my latest story. She was not happy at all. She wanted me to dial 911 and go to the emergency room.

I told her, "No, I will leave the motorcycle here at my work. I already called a taxi to take me to the airport. I am coming home."

"Okay. Let me know when you get to the airport. I will get you on the next flight I can and get you home."

Defeated, I said, "I will. I think the World has spoken. It just is not good for me to be alone. How many more signs do I need?"

She said, "We will get you home, find a doctor, and see what happened. Okay? How long will it be for the taxi?"

"Hopefully, not much longer. I just want to get out of here," I said

Worried, Kim replied, "I'll talk with you until the taxi comes if you want."

"It's okay, thanks. I better walk out to the gate, so he can find me. He can't get in here anyway."

The taxi finally showed up and took me to the airport. Even though the pain was excruciating, I somehow made it into the airport. I got my boarding pass and settled onto the last flight to Poison Oak International Airport. I found a seat on the plane and collapsed.

## Thoughts of Alcohol

At least I was going home. If I could have, I would have drunk any alcoholic drink Southwest had to offer. These thoughts had been going through my mind even more since the loss of Jeffrey. It had been over eight years since I had a drink, but the thought of not feeling anything appealed to me increasingly more often.

Between the physical pain of my injury and the mental pain of my life, being numb would have been a blessing. However, this would not have been the right time to take that first drink. Bud and Jeffrey were so proud of me when I quit drinking.

If I started again, I knew they would both be disappointed, so I resigned myself to rest for the short flight home. I closed my eyes and put my head back, which was not easy with the amount of pain I was in. I decided I was not going to sit in an emergency room all night.

Kim picked me up in Poison Oak, California. She believed I should go directly to an emergency room. I just wanted to get home, so I promised to seek medical treatment in the morning.

After we got home, Kim put ice on my injured areas for a while. I went to bed for the night. When I woke up the next morning, I was still in extreme pain. I could not move my right arm at all. Kim found a doctor who could see me right away. His name was Dr. Murphy in Waterville, California.

**Medical Evaluations**

Even though Kim was not a fan of chiropractors, she knew I was not going to go sit in an emergency room for hours. I knew nothing broke; it felt like I pulled a muscle. I had seen chiropractors before and hoped Dr. Murphy would be able to relieve my pain.

He took X-rays and confirmed nothing broke. He performed an adjustment to my spine and neck. He applied stem therapy along with an ultrasound treatment to my shoulder and neck. He told me to alternate ice and heat for the rest of the weekend and made an appointment for Monday.

# Workman's Comp Claim

On Monday morning, I called my work and gave an official report of the injury of July 26. What a whopper of a day the 26$^{th}$ of July turned out to be. A blown front tire and an injury. What was the World trying to tell me?

Medical treatment for my injury became complicated as I lived in California. I drove out of Utah, and the company corporate offices were in Maine. Thankfully, they agreed I could receive medical treatment in California.

July 26, 2001 was the last day I ever drove a tractor-trailer. The company officially put me out on workers' compensation. Driving a truck had been my career for over a decade. I loved driving professionally. It allowed me to raise my two sons in a manner that gave them all the things they needed and wanted. I not only enjoyed the job, the travel, the friendship with the other drivers, but I cherished the freedom and time alone it gave me.

Losing my career hit me hard. As another loss, it knocked me down even farther. I walked down to the beach. Sitting there, I contemplated how my life had changed so quickly. It was truly incredible all the things that happened in such a brief time. From March 26 to July 26, my world twisted upside down and inside out.

# Blessings

I tried to find a blessing in the nightmare of my life. The first blessing I could think of was thankfully, the Universe brought me Kim before They took Jeffrey. The second blessing was that Bud came home before They took Jeffrey. I doubt either Bud or I would have made it through this tragedy had we not been together.

Kim strengthened our family with love, compassion, and kindness. It was extremely hard for me to believe and trust that somebody would stay in my life and love me. All my life, people had always made promises of this and that, but they never fulfilled their promises.

From the time my sons were born, we were the Three Musketeers. It was unbelievable that the Three Musketeers had become Two of a Kind. Bud and I would figure out how to survive. We had to be there for each other for the rest of our lives. We needed each other.

The Next Day Came. No matter what happened, the damn thing kept coming.

CHAPTER 41

# DOCTORS AND MORE DOCTORS

Was the World out to get me? My thought patterns scattered, and the direction was not good. Dr. Murphy continued to treat my injuries. However, my arm did not seem to heal. He ordered an MRI, but the results were inconclusive. The diagnosis was frozen shoulder. I lost 95 percent of my right arm's range of motion.

It became impossible for me to raise my arm up or to reach out. To fix this, the doctors put me under anesthesia three days in a row and tore the scar tissue in my shoulder to get the arm moving again. Then, I painfully started therapy all over again.

I saw Dr. Arrow, my primary doctor, and she was extremely concerned about my health. Since the murder of Jeffrey in March, I had suffered from uncontrollable migraines. I had never experienced a migraine before in my life.

Dr. Arrow believed the shock and stress of Jeffrey's murder triggered the migraines. They were so extreme Dr. Arrow prescribed an emergency shot that I jabbed into my thigh, like an epi-pen for bee stings. The migraine pain was excruciating, and I suffered from five or more migraines a week.

During those migraines, I experienced extreme pain and nausea, all at the same time. I could not stand bright light or loud noises. I knew from stories that Melinda suffered horribly from migraines as a teenager.

Since I was not speaking to my mother, after her behavior at the announcement of Jeffrey's murder, I would not ask her details about her condition as a child.

Dr. Arrow said, "The migraines could be hereditary, but I honestly believe your migraines are stress-related."

## Brownies and New Friends

The medical conditions escalated. My blood pressure was high. I did not sleep. I hardly ate. If I ate, I did not eat a brownie—it was a pan of brownies.

Here is a funny story. When we moved into the townhouses, we met our neighbor, Betty. She and I were quite the pair as we were both depressed and anti-social.

Betty had recently gone through a horrible divorce, and I had lost my son to homicide. This was how we became great friends. It began one day when Kim was traveling, and I wanted brownies. I knocked on Betty's door.

I asked, "Betty, do you know how to make brownies? Kim is not home, and I need some."

"Well, it's been years, but I'll give it a try," she answered.

Our friendship developed from that day forward. If Kim was out of town for work, Betty made me brownies. We shared dozens of brownies. The brownies turned out not to be a good thing for my health. Type II Diabetes was my next diagnosis, but I could have cared less. In fact, I wished I would die. I could not picture a better way to die than eating pans of brownies.

## Mental Health and Psychiatrists

Dr. Arrow disagreed with my opinion and was concerned with my mental state of mind. I was a mess, in a deep depression; life became more than I could manage. Dr. Arrow recommended I speak with a psychiatrist.

Kim found a wonderful psychiatrist named Dr. Carston. Her practice was just down the road from our townhouse in Otter Beach. Amazingly, I managed to get myself there all by myself.

Dr. Carston was an officer and medical doctor in the Army Reserves. She specialized in parents who had lost a child and worked with military families. I fit both of her specialties. Bud was in the military, and I lost a child.

G.I. Ranger and I had attended marriage counseling in Hawaii, but this was different. I had taken Jeffrey to a couple of psychiatrists, but I had never been to a psychiatrist before. However, I felt comfortable with Dr. Carston from the start.

On our first visit, I told her Jeffrey's story, the whole nightmare. I explained the odd appearance of Artie and Gail, Jeffrey's father. I told her how I found out they were having an affair when I was eight months pregnant with Jeffrey, which resulted in my divorce from Artie.

I shared the unbelievable event of going to the House of Murder. We talked about the sentencing hearing, and what a horrible experience it was to see and stand in front of the man who murdered my child. I described how horrible it was for Bud, yet how proud I was of him. He had faced his anger and honored Jeffrey. I also related the encounter with Jack Ashe's mother.

I described the Huge Expensive Vacation that was originally meant for me. Then, I finished off with all the illnesses I acquired, and the calamities that had happened at work since Jeffrey's murder. I described my injury and the probability of not being able to return to my profession.

## Help for Bud Too

We talked about Bud. I explained how close he and Jeffrey were. She thought it was amazing that they were born on the same date. I told her Bud was struggling with the loss of Jeffrey and shared my diagnosis that he was suffering from survivors' guilt.

Dr. Carston said, "Bud can come to a couple of appointments with you."

She understood he did not want to go to a psychiatrist and have it on his military records. Bud needed somebody to talk to so he could move forward through the loss of Jeffrey. He only went with me a couple of times, but it truly helped him to understand it was not his fault somebody murdered Jeffrey.

I found out through her and other military people there could be adverse effects for people in the military if they looked for psychiatric or mental health care. This includes issues, such as: depression, anger, post-traumatic stress disorder (PTSD), or suicidal thoughts. These visits could result in disqualification for promotions and re-enlistment opportunities.

## Suicidal Thoughts and Lies

I was thankful Dr. Carston understood the situation. Mere words could not describe all the horrors I shared with Dr. Carston. Concerned about my mental state of mind, she thought I might be suicidal. *Good catch on her part*—because truthfully, I was extremely suicidal, but I would not tell her, or anyone, the truth.

I do not recommend for anyone to lie, but I knew if I told her I was suicidal; she would commit me to a hospital for evaluation. I was not going to the hospital, period. She could have *Baker Acted* me, as they called it in California. I did not want to go to a hospital against my will. I lied, "No, I have to stick around and help Bud."

She seemed relieved with that statement but made me promise her that I would call her if that changed.

I said, "I promise I will call you if I need to." Then I asked, "Could I have changed the outcome of my child's death?"

Dr. Carston pointed out one thing that really helped me. She said, "Everything you are thinking, and feeling is normal."

This comforted me, as I genuinely thought I was losing my mind. I told her, "I thought I would die, but I have not. I spend most days playing the game, *would have, could have, and should have* in my head."

Dr. Carston told me, "You can play those games forever, and it will never change what happened."

I answered, "I know that, but it doesn't stop it from happening."

**Helpful Book**

She said, "I have a book I want you to read; I think it will help you. I think it will give you a sense of peace. It explains your child came here for a reason, he completed that reason, and then he went home."

I looked at her in disbelief. I never heard that before. I asked her, "Do you believe that?"

She said, "Yes, I do. The book is called *Embraced by the Light,* by Betty Eadie."

"Okay, I'll get it today."

"Please try to read it by our next appointment. We can talk about it then."

"I doubt anything will ever give me peace," I said.

She said, "Take all this information with a grain of salt. Nothing compares to the loss of a child. You gave eighteen years, sacrificed for him, and nurtured him to get him to adulthood. Then somebody murdered him, violently and needlessly."

"Exactly. There is a hole in my soul; it is like part of me is missing."

## You Are Normal

Dr. Carston continued, "You will laugh, then you will cry. You will be angry. You will yell and even scream. You may have to punch or kick things. You may not sleep, and when you do sleep, you may suffer nightmares. Just know that all of this is normal."

I said, "All these things happened to me in the last few months."

"I am not surprised at all," replied Dr. Carston.

I asked, "Will I ever get better? Will I ever get over the loss of my child?"

She replied, "You will not necessarily get over it, but you will come to a Different Place. Brokenhearted, you will find peace. You will forever miss your child. Just know that there are no quick fixes. It will take time, a lot of time, but you will find a new peace, and a new purpose."

"He was my best friend," I cried.

She said, "You are going to make it, Kathy. You have important things to live for. You need to help Bud succeed in his life. You have support from Kim. Someday, please write a book, tell this story, and share it with others. Your knowledge and experience will help them through the same unbelievably painful process that you survived."

I am sure I looked at her disbelievingly. I replied, "Okay, if you say so. I will take your word for it."

## Diagnoses and Medications

Dr. Carston diagnosed me with post-traumatic stress disorder (PTSD) and a condition called complicated grief.

She said, "Complicated grief is more intense and painful than normal grief. This condition happens mostly to women." She continued, "I am going to prescribe an antidepressant and an anti-anxiety medication. These medications will settle you down and help you find a balance. Too many things have gone wrong in your life, all at one time."

I told her, "I have not had a drink for eight years now. I would not start to drink again and dishonor Bud and Jeffrey. I only do prescription drugs, and the doctors have me on way too many of them, what's two more?"

Dr. Carston was impressed I had stayed sober. "Let's talk more next week. I'll see you then."

There were thousands of tears shed while I visited Dr. Carston's office. With her, I did not have to be the strong one or have any of the answers. I could just hurt, be sad, and depressed with her. I was the mom who lost her baby boy.

On my way home, I picked up the book that Dr. Carston recommended, *Embraced by the Light*, by Betty Eadie. I read it straight through that night. I quickly realized why Dr. Carston wanted me to read it. It gave me a new understanding about life and death.

The story gave me peace, knowing that Jeffrey came into my life for a reason. He chose to be my child. He completed the reason he came to Earth for, and then he went home to a better place. The best part of the book for me was that he would be waiting for me when I died. This gave me hope.

Reading this book gave me peace and comfort. I knew Jeffrey touched dozens of people's lives while he was here on Earth. He saved my life more than a hundred times when I was sad, depressed, or even suicidal. He made people believe things would get better and inspired them to hang on.

Jeffrey was a healer, a kind and gentle soul. He always shared a hug and a kiss with me or anyone that needed it. Jeffrey blessed my life in so many ways. His love helped me learn to love and be a better mother to both my children.

The Next Day Came. The days continued to come whether I wanted them to or not.

## CHAPTER 42

# PROMISES MADE

Another month passed after the murder of Jeffrey. At least the large black bird continued to make an appearance every day. I felt like the bird came just to check on me, and make sure I was doing okay. Still lost and confused, I tried every day to dig my way out of the nightmare and depression.

Drifting in a sea of darkness with no work, a murdered child, and in extreme pain, I could see no way out of the hell my life had become. My depression deepened daily. It felt like I ran up the down escalator all day long. I went nowhere fast. It took everything I had to drag myself to doctor appointments.

My life had changed so drastically in such a brief time. Even worse, I was home alone quite often as Kim traveled regularly for work. My life for twenty-two years had been about raising my two sons, which included surviving as a single parent and gainful employment. Suddenly, I could no longer work. For eighteen years, I had worked; not working really frightened me.

**Called on My Promises**

Thankfully, Bud was doing better than me. He had the Navy, school, and work to distract him. Bud came home one day and saw how depressed I was and how I struggled. He decided to straighten my attitude out, as he called it.

Bud reminded me of something I preached on to him and Jeffrey throughout their childhood.

"Mom, remember what you always told Jeffrey and me?" Bud asked.

"No, what are you talking about, Bud?"

"You promised us that when we grew up, you would go to college. You said you would get a degree so you could find an easier job. Right?"

"Yes, I might have said that Bud." I conceded.

He looked at me, smiled, and pointed at himself. "Well, Mom, in case you haven't noticed, we grew up."

"Pay back's a bitch, right, Bud?"

"Yep, that's right, Mom!"

**Dysfunctional Families**

Bud had grown up to be just like me. He was correct. I told them hundreds of times that if they had an education, they could do anything. An education gives people choices in life. I told them how smart and handsome they were. I made sure they believed they could do anything and be whatever they wanted to be.

Raised in a dysfunctional home, I made sure my children did not learn the same inferiority complexes I suffered from. My boys heard all the things I never heard growing up.

I said, "I also told you that you could prove people right, or you could prove people wrong. You and Jeffrey proved everyone wrong."

My family said that Bud and Jeffrey would never amount to anything. This was something that my father said to me as a child. I wanted to make sure my children knew they had options either way.

Well, Bud threw my own advice right back at me. Bud said, "Mom, why don't you go to college?"

"Bud, how am I supposed to go to college? I'm not even working now."

"This would be a perfect time, wouldn't it? You keep complaining about having nothing to do," he answered.

"Bud, I don't know the first thing about going to college."

Bud laughed at me. He said, "Well, let me help you. This is what I do for the veterans at the college. First, go online and fill out the free application for federal student aid (FAFSA). This will help you see if you qualify for a Pell Grant or a student loan."

Reluctantly, I said, "I suppose I could probably do that."

He continued, "After that, go down to Surf City College and get a catalog for the fall courses. See what classes you might be interested in. This will be fun. We could go to college together."

I was still doubtful. I asked, "What classes would I take?"

He laughed and said, "I don't know. What classes interest you? I am sure Kim can help you figure it out. She has a master's degree in business administration, an MBA." He stressed: M–B–A.

"Okay Bud, I'll ask her what she thinks when she gets home. I guess you did grow up, just like your mother, into a smart ass."

I asked myself: *Did I promise two little boys that when they grew up, I would go to college?*

Truthfully, I do not remember. Either way, Bud called me on it, so I had to stand up to it. The pressure was on me. I would have to talk to Kim about it. The Promise I made came back to bite me in the ass.

## Marisol's Help

I needed more information, so I called Marisol. She had gotten a job in financial aid back in March. I figured she would be able to tell me about this FAFSA thing. Marisol laughed when I told her the story.

Marisol said, "Bud told me that story many times, about how you promised to go to college when they grew up. He is so proud of you. He says you are his inspiration in life."

"Wow, Bud said that about me?"

"Yes, he's said that many times," Marisol said.

"Wow, how cool is that? He is such a good boy," I said proudly.

"So, just google FAFSA and fill out the application. You will not be able to receive financial aid until next year. It's too late for this year. The application must be in by March for the following year."

"Thanks," I said. "Okay, I will fill it out. I guess I can start with a couple of classes."

Marisol agreed, "Absolutely you can; that would be great. You need to go down and get a California identification card too. That way, next year, you will not have to pay out-of-state tuition."

I replied, "Okay, thanks for all the advice. Kim will be shocked when she gets home."

Marisol laughed, "That's for sure. Go down and get a catalog at the bookstore. Then look through it. See what classes you might like to take."

I laughed and said, "Yeah, that's what Bud said. I have no idea what I want to do when I grow up. I'd have to grow up first."

Marisol said, "You'll do fine. Let me know if I can do anything else to help."

"I will do that. Thanks! Love you."

Surf City College, what was I thinking? I figured out the parking procedures. I asked for directions to the bookstore. I asked the clerk where I would find the fall catalog. I found it; surprisingly, it was free. I took two catalogs and headed back to my car. I could not wait for Kim to call. I was excited to tell her the news.

**Surprise and Shock**

To my surprise, I thought about something besides murders and injuries. I might even have something to look forward to. What a change from the events of the previous five months. Kim called later that evening.

Kim said, "Hey, what's going on? You sound peppy."

"Well, you'd better sit down," I said.

Instantly worried, she said, "Oh Geez, you are making me nervous. Now what?"

I laughed, "No, it's good news this time."

"Oh, thank god, we've had enough bad news to last a lifetime."

I said, "Bud saw me moping around today. He decided I should go to college with him. He told me I Promised him and Jeffrey."

Excitedly, Kim said, "Wow, what do you think about it?"

I replied, "Well, I went down and picked up a fall catalog at Surf City College. Bud said you could help me pick out some classes."

Kim laughed, "He volunteered me to help you pick out classes?"

"Yes, he said you have an M-B-A and would be able to help me. He is quite impressed with that MBA, I might add."

Laughing, Kim said, "That is hilarious. Absolutely, I will help you. That Bud is a smart boy."

Kim would not be home for another day, so I thought I would look at the catalog. Wow, I was not ready for college. The book looked complicated. It had things about pre-requisites. I was not sure where to even start. I put the book up. I decided to wait for Kim. I would not say the words, but I thought: *Could things be okay?*

Dr. Carston said, "I would never be the same again, but I would come to a Different Place."

Would going to college be my Different Place?

**College Decisions**

Kim arrived home from her work travels, and I gave her time to settle in. It was hard to believe, but I was excited about something. I thought, *this college thing could be a good for me.*

At least I would have something to do, something different to occupy my mind. I got the catalog out, and we flipped through the pages. There were a hundred classes starting at various times, and dozens of them required pre-requisites. I was not sure what that even meant.

# Kim's Favorite Story About Me

Kim said, "Why don't you start with a history class? You like history. Here is an art history class."

I replied, "I can't take that. I don't know anything about art history."

Kim tried again. "Okay, how about taking a foreign language class? You always say that you want to learn Spanish."

I replied, "I can't take Spanish. I don't know anything about speaking Spanish."

You get the picture, right? It went back and forth, and the frustration level rose on both sides. My perfectionism reared its ugly head. I demanded, "How am I supposed to take a class about something I know nothing about?"

Kim looked at me like I had two heads. "The whole point of going to college is to learn about new things."

Frustrated, I said, "Maybe this isn't a promising idea. I can't do this. I can't go to school and appear stupid. Besides, it has been years since I was in high school. I probably don't remember all that stupid stuff I learned."

Kim laughed, "You are one of the smartest people I've ever met. I know you will do fine going back to school."

"I have to start taking classes. Bud believed me when I said I would go to college when he and Jeffrey grew up. I'll start with a class or two and see what happens."

Kim agreed, "The most important thing you can do right now is to keep moving forward. Bud needs to see you moving forward, so he can too. Keep the promises you made to him and Jeffrey. You know how much Bud looks up to you."

Being a mom was one tough job, especially a mom who lost a child. If I was strong, then Bud would be strong too. I signed up for college and did everything possible to make Bud and Jeffrey proud of me. I learned that by living the life I wanted Bud to live, I set a good example for Bud.

Bud and I moved forward slowly. Together, we made Jeffrey proud of us. We attended college for Jeffrey, in his honor. Jeffrey could not be here with us, but I knew he watched us from heaven.

**Off to College, I Go**

So, that was how my college education started on August 26, 2001. Another 26 in the pattern. Things changed after all. Finally, a good thing happened. I started college as I Promised my sons. Next stop: a degree and that easier job.

Never one to do anything half-assed, I jumped into college with both feet. I told Kim I would sign up for a couple classes, but my first semester at Surf City College began with six classes: Spanish, Survey of Business, Career Planning, Interpersonal Communication, Word, and Excel. Thankfully, the computer classes would be a refresher for me as I had experience using Microsoft Office.

Nervous about starting college, I arrived early to the campus. Raised by a Marine Corp sergeant, being early was not a surprise. My father said, "To be early is to be on time, to be on time is to be late, and to be late is unforgivable."

Things started out with a bang on my first day. I learned quickly that parking on the first day of the semester was virtually impossible. However, it became clear quickly that parking got easier every day of the semester. People stopped going to school all the time. This phenomenon confused me as people paid for classes, but then they did not show up.

## Talking to Myself

Arriving early, I found a spot quickly. With a map and a room number in hand, I was off to my first class in college. It could not be that complicated, could it? I found the classroom, went into the class, and sat down.

I said aloud, "Okay, not too bad. This college stuff was not so tough. I should have signed up for a class with Bud. He would have helped me and given me moral support."

Once again, my father's Marine Corps voice popped into my head. "Buck up, stupid. You can do this."

Other students came into the classroom and sat down.

I said aloud, "How many years has it been since I was in high school? These kids look like they were about twelve years old. Wait until I tell Kim about this one."

I found the habit of talking to myself had increased exponentially since the death of Jeffrey. He and I used to talk to each other all the time, and I missed that, so I just talked to myself. I made a note to ask Dr. Carston about this dilemma.

Gosh, I felt old at forty. Bud and Jeffrey were the same age as these students. Suddenly, it dawned on me I was old enough to be these kids' mother. I wished Bud and Jeffrey could have been there with me to share this moment. I know they were proud of me.

## First Class–Beginning Spanish

The classroom filled up quickly, and finally, a woman closer to my age walked through the door. She was the most Asian woman I had ever seen.

I said aloud, "Oh great, my first day and I'm in the wrong classroom."

I often tell people I need expert advice, so I talk to myself. They usually do not see the humor in this saying. Anyway, I pulled out my class schedule, double-checked the course, and room number where I was supposed to be.

I got up and walked out into the hall and checked the door number. Yes, this was the correct place, according to my paperwork. I walked back into the room. The professor must have seen my confusion.

The professor asked, "Are you supposed to be in Beginning Spanish?"

"Yes."

"You are in the correct place. Have a seat."

She introduced herself. "My name is Dr. Gonzaga. I am the instructor for Beginning Spanish. I am from Peru. My mother is Peruvian. My father's family came to Peru from Japan, so I am also Japanese, and I take after my father."

Nobody said a word; everybody continued to stare at her.

"The Japanese came as workers to Peru to help build my country, much like they did from Japan to the United States. I speak both fluent Spanish and Japanese. I am thrilled to have you in my classroom. I hope to have a lot of fun this semester teaching you to love the Spanish language."

Dr. Gonzaga became a mentor to me through my year and a half at Surf City College. We became close friends. I shared the story of the murder of Jeffrey and how I ended up in her class through a Promise made to two little boys. She loved that I attended college in Jeffrey's honor, fulfilling The Promise I made to Bud and Jeffrey.

Dr. Gonzaga was influential in teaching me I had the ability to not only learn, but to excel in my college career. I received an associate degree at Surf City College in December 2002. Following is an excerpt from a letter of recommendation written by Dr. Gonzaga, PhD:

> Throughout the life of a teacher, there are always those students who leave a mark on the teacher's mind. Kathy is one of those students. Her spirit of determination to start a new career and overcome academic, health, and personal challenges have been admirable. Her sense of discipline, completion, and achievement, along with her zest to learn the new and the different, and to be of service to society, places her among the best student candidates for your program. I am honored to have her in my classes.

Dr. Gonzaga's words meant the world to me. I cannot recall anyone saying such kind things about me. This encouragement and recognition from her gave me hope that I could make it through the loss of Jeffrey, albeit in a completely Different Place than I ever thought possible.

CHAPTER 43

# LESSONS LEARNED

Dr. Carston taught me lessons I carry with me today. The biggest one was there are always losses in life. She explained that a loss is a loss; it does not matter what that loss is. To the person who experiences the loss, it is traumatic. She believed that anyone who suffered a loss should seek counseling.

Dr. Carston taught me that death does not make an appointment, and it comes to everyone eventually. When experiencing these types of losses, people should seek psychiatric help, especially with the loss of a child. A loss of a child is particularly traumatic to a mother and often causes complicated grief. She said, "The loss could be a child or a loved one, a job, a big client, a marriage, or even a pet. No matter what the loss, the person must move through that loss to heal, or they will get stuck, and that is a horrible place to be. I guarantee you, Kathy, it is always harder to lose a child."

During every visit, Dr. Carston encouraged me to write and talk about my story. She believed it would help other people. Dr. Carston wanted other people to see that I went through hell, yet I kept The Promise I made to my children. She said, "Kathy, reading your story will give people hope. Look how reading the book I told you to read gave you hope."

"Yes, Dr. Carston, it did. I deeply appreciated it."

Dr. Carston recognized hope was what people needed to survive, especially a parent. They need to know there is life after the loss of a child. She said, "You not only survived, but you thrived by honoring your child. You fulfilled the promises you made to him as a child and got him through high school. Your child is forever in your heart, soul, and mind. Please talk about your loss. Live life and do the things your child can no longer do. Make him proud of you every day, in everything you do and say."

I took this to heart. I went home and told Bud what she said. Bud and I made a pact that very moment. This became the way we lived our lives every single day.

Dr. Carston also taught me that people are afraid of death. She said, "Societal norms are not to talk about death. People believe they are being kind when they avoid talking about the dead."

"I disagree," I said. "To say the wrong thing is better than saying nothing."

**Loss of Family and Friends**

When I lost my child, I received a double whammy because I lost the rest of my family too. My parents never talked about the loss of my child. They died half a dozen years later. Even stranger, my extended family no longer speak to me either. If it were not for Facebook, I would not know what they were doing, or even if they were alive.

I contemplated this dilemma for years. After a person's life is destroyed by the loss of a child, or a devastating loss of any kind, what reason could people have for hurting that person in extreme pain, depression, and anger even more?

Did they fear it would hurt the persons feelings? Did they think death was contagious, or by associating with the person who lost a child, their child would die too? Did they think death hung on us and gave the power to curse their world?

I researched this phenomenon and conducted over a hundred interviews with other people who lost a child or loved one.

1. They feel alone, avoided, and ignored by family members and friends.
2. Family members grew tired of hearing about the deceased loved one.
3. They became pariahs and avoided by people who knew them.
4. People no longer mentioned their child or loved one's name.
5. It was as if their child or loved one never existed.

These answers repeated in every interview. I concluded that people do not know what to say, so they say nothing.

**Questions Asked–Left Unanswered**

I asked for input from my family and extended family on anything they remembered about Jeffrey and his life. The first time I asked, I received one response.

Lynette said, "Lea came with me to the terminal to pick you up, and all my children and grandchildren went to the funeral home."

The second time I asked, I got one response.

Lynette said, "That is just too sad to think about."

I often wonder what people envision my life to be like every single day. My days consist of thoughts about Jeffrey, the loss of Jeffrey, and all the things I would never get to share with Jeffrey again. I talk to him, tell him how I miss him, and how very much I love him.

How could it be sadder for them than it was for me? Really?

Let me say I hope nobody ever finds themselves in the situation I ended up in. If you are a family member, friend, or a loved one, of a person who lost a loved one, especially a child, please take this advice.

1. Speak their name. We remember the loss with every breath we take.
2. Tell funny stories that you remember about their lost loved one.
3. Do not hide from them; they are not contagious.
4. Say anything; it is way better than saying nothing.
5. A mother never gets over the loss of a child.

As for me:

6. You will not offend me. I have not forgotten my child.
7. You will not hurt my feelings if you talk about Jeffrey.

Dr. Carston and I saw each other for six months. The information and skills she shared helped me immensely. I struggled for the longest time with finding my purpose. For so many years, my job was to raise my two boys to be good adults, and I did that.

I believed Bud would be okay whether I was around for him or not. He was like me, before the murder of Jeffrey. He was strong, and there were so many things he wanted to do. I do not know if that was true or not, but in my mind, I rationalized it.

The only reason I quit seeing Dr. Carston was we moved from Captain Island to Frostbite, California. Continuing to see her would have been impossible with a three-hour drive, one way.

I missed our weekly talks, but she convinced me I would be okay, someday! I could learn to live my life again, even laugh and have fun, albeit in a completely Different Place than it was before. That day could not come soon enough. I can honestly say that Dr. Carston *saved my life*.

The Next Day Came. It continued to come.

# CONCLUSION

Jeffrey's murder changed how we thought and how we lived our lives. One thing Dr. Carston told me that gave me peace about Jeffrey's death was her belief about death. She convinced me that when it was your turn to go, you went. It did not matter where you were; you would die.

My only wish is that Jeffrey had not been so violently murdered. The thought of this bothers me and makes my heart sad. When I hear about a murder on television news, I always hear that people need or want to get closure.

My wisdom on this subject is that no matter what happened to the perpetrator who murdered your child or loved one, it will never bring your child or loved one back. I found absolutely no closure in Jack Ashe's plea bargain or his time in prison.

From my experience, the victim's family became blessed if the police kill the perpetrator, or the perpetrator kills themselves. The death of the perpetrator saves the family continuing agony after the loss of their loved one.

You might think this cold but imagine the pain of hearing how your loved one suffered or died every day, day after day. The story of Jeffrey's murder in a robbery constantly appeared on the television news and in the newspapers. Next, it was in the courtroom. It only extended the horror of the situation.

To speak at the sentencing hearing brought forth immeasurable agony of what would *never* be: no weddings, no grandchildren, no holidays, no birthdays, nor vacations. Even with a conviction, I did not find closure. No matter the outcome of any trial, loved ones never come back to life.

It is torture to have the person who killed their loved one still alive. That person will be watching television, playing cards, or talking with friends. They can take classes and receive a college education. These are all the things their loved one will never experience. These thoughts never leave the family's minds. There truly is no such thing as closure.

## The Next Day Comes

Bud gave me a new purpose, a mission, and The Promise to keep. I had something to focus on. I needed to fulfill The Promise I made to him and Jeffrey all those years ago. That Promise, and that Promise alone, kept me focused on my purpose every single day.

Every day, I got up, went to my classes, completed my homework, and worked towards the degree I promised those two little boys I would get. Besides, someday, I wanted to find out what that easier job was that I would get with that college education.

When the Next Day Came, and I woke up once again, I lived that day with the sole purpose of making my two sons proud of me. I believed in my heart that Jeffrey was always proud of me up in heaven.

Jeffrey watched over me. He guided me in all that I did. When I was down or scared, I remembered all the times in my life he helped me to be a better person.

Bud and I treasured Jeffrey's love for life. He taught us so many things as he grew up. I do not know how to put into words the kindness and understanding that Jeffrey exuded beyond his age. He truly was an old soul.

I always said, "Jeffrey was four, going on forty."

## One Final Observation

This went around and around in my mind for years, but I found it interesting. I never truly understood it until after Jeffrey's death. The story goes, from the time Jeffrey could talk, he always said these words. "I cannot wait until I am eighteen."

There was never any context or consistency of when or why he said these words. He just randomly announced them, quite boldly. I could not tell you the hundreds of times I heard Jeffrey say those words.

As his mother, I thought he just wanted to be a grownup, an adult. I thought he wanted to be on his own, live by his own rules, and be able to do whatever he wanted. The truth of what he said became clear to me after his murder.

I thought I figured it out, but I wanted confirmation of my conclusion, so I went to a local psychic that a friend recommended. I asked her if she could confirm what I thought was correct. I told her the story, and she agreed that Jeffrey knew he would die at the age of eighteen. We both believed Jeffrey recognized that at eighteen, he would die and *go home*, or whatever you choose to call it. He truly could not wait to get there.

The psychic said, "Jeffrey believed he could help you more from the other side then he could from this side at this point in your life. He watches over you all the time, and if you pay attention, you will see signs he is nearby. He likes to come as a bird and check in on you. He loves to fly free. Keep an eye out and you will see him. He loves you very much and is extremely proud of you and all you have done at school."

It finally made sense to me. I was happy for Jeffrey, and I even had a sense of peace. Even though I missed him terribly with every breath I took, I knew in my heart he found the peace he waited eighteen years to achieve.

Jeffrey's presence surrounded Bud and me as he watched over us, protected us, and guided us to our new purposes. Bud and I would forever miss Jeffrey. The world seemed a much more empty, lonely place without him.

Bud and I spent hours sharing funny stories about Jeffrey. We also shared his silliness, kindness, and love of life. He brought such joy and laughter into our lives. His love for people and animals continued to fill our hearts. With his loss, our lives changed forever.

Bud and I worked together to find our new paths. We learned painfully that life was ambiguous. Neither of us could have imagined the changes that came into our lives. Bud and I found a way to survive as *Two of a Kind*.

Our story continues in the next book of *The Next Day Came* Trilogy: *Bud—Homicide Turns a Mother's Blue Star Gold*.

# NEXT STEPS

Now that you read *Jeffrey, it is time to learn the rest of story.* Read all three books in *The Next Day Came Trilogy*.

**Book One:** *Jeffrey — A Mother Encounters the Injustice of Murder*

**Book Two:** *Bud — Homicide Turns A Mother's Blue Star Gold* (Release Date 2021)

**Book Three:** *Kathy — A Mother's Journey Through Tragic Loss* (Release Date 2021)

Find these books:

eBook / Paperback / Audio: amazon.com/K-D-Wagner/e/B08D7T1HHM/
Autographed hardcover:   www.kdwagner.com

In Book One, *Jeffrey*, you found hope in loss and suggestions for moving forward. K. D. Wagner can support you—or someone you know—on the journey.

**Special Offers:**

1. *Find Your Purpose After Loss* group
2. *Don't Get Lost in Your Loss* program
3. *Personal Mentoring* with K. D. Wagner

   **Sign up** here for these offers: www.kdwagner.com

To **book** K. D. Wagner for a speaking engagement, contact us at www.kdwagner.com.

**Text** the word KDWAGNER to 64600 for more information.

**Email** the author at meetme@kdwagner.com

- ✓ *Take more photos of your children and loved ones. You will never have enough!*
- ✓ *There is not a word for a parent that loses a child, but there is an organization that supports families of lost children. A donation for 5% of all book proceeds will go to The American Gold Star Mothers, Inc., Gulf Coast Chapter.*
- ✓ *Donate directly to The American Gold Star Mothers, Inc., Gulf Coast Chapter to support Veterans Families who have lost a loved one at* www.kdwagner.com

# ABOUT THE AUTHOR

K. D. Wagner is an international speaker and a #1 International bestselling author featured in How Big Can You Dream? and Raising the Bar Volume 3. Her Trilogy, *The Next Day Came*, reveals her journey through depression, addiction, planned suicide, and survival after the unimaginable violent loss of her two sons in separate homicides, two years apart. Ironically, K. D. previously served as a law enforcement officer.

K. D. Wagner is a Gold Star Mother because her oldest son, died while serving on active duty in the U.S. Navy during Operation Iraqi Freedom. She serves as the Vice President of her local chapter. Her volunteerism supports veterans, their families, and the community. She speaks on their behalf, promotes awareness, and raises contributions for their organization.

Wagner has traveled the world, helping hundreds of people on the topics of loss, survival, and thriving. She speaks on the loss of a child, gun violence, grief, addiction, learning disabilities and how to move forward with strength and courage. With profound empathy, K. D. Wagner inspires people to find the purpose in their pain and to convert that purpose into a new passion for life.

K. D. Wagner earned both a bachelor's and master's degree in Criminal Justice from California State University with highest honors to fulfill The Promise, and in Honor of her two sons.

She has appeared on NBC News and on stages with the Joint Chief of Staff General Mark Milley, Governor Rick Scott, Rock Legend Alice Cooper, Country Singer Rockie Lynne, Bob Circosta of the *Home Shopping Network*, Nancy Matthews of the *Women's Prosperity Network*, Dr. Lydie Louis Esq, Orly Amor, Gary Coxe, Matt Bacak, J.T. Foxx, AmondaRose Igoe, and Shannon Gronich of the *Business Acceleration Network*.

K. D. Wagner took the Leap of Faith and *jumped* at 14,000 feet with the U.S. Army Elite Parachute Team—The Golden Knights and *bent steel* with Bert Oliva. In her journey, she has discovered ways to not only survive, but to thrive under extreme circumstances.

K. D. Wagner's mission is to honor her sons in everything she does, and to be the person they believe her to be. Her purpose is to inspire others to find their strength to transition into a new powerful and fulfilled life.

K. D. currently resides in Florida with her spouse, Kim, and their standard poodles.